MANAGING YOUR PRIORITIES FROM START TO SUCCESS

MANAGING YOUR PRIORITIES FROM START TO SUCCESS

William J. Bond

IRWIN
Professional Publishing®
Chicago • London • Singapore

The Briefcase Books Series

The Briefcase Books Series

Research shows that people who buy business books (1) want books that can be read quickly, perhaps on a plane trip, commuting on a train, or overnight, and (2) feel their time and money were well spent if they get two or three useful insights or techniques for improving their professional skills or helping them with a current problem at work.

Briefcase Books were designed to meet these two criteria. They focus on necessary skills and problem areas, and include real-world examples from practicing managers and professionals. Inside these books you'll find useful, practical information and techniques in a straightforward, concise, and easy-to-read format.

This book and others like it in the Briefcase Books series can quickly give you insights and answers regarding your current needs and problems. And they are useful references for future situations and problems.

If you find this book or any other in this series to be of value, please share it with your co-workers. With tens of thousands of new books published each year, any book that can simplify the growing complexities in managing others needs to be circulated as widely as possible.

Robert B. Nelson
Series Editor

Times Mirror
Higher Education Group

Library of Congress Cataloging-in-Publication Data

Bond, William J.
  Managing your priorities from start to success / William J. Bond.
    p.   cm. — (The briefcase books series)
  Includes index.
  ISBN 0–7863–0387–5
  1. Strategic planning.   2. Time management.   3. Success in business.
  4. Success.   I. Title.   II. Series.
  HD30.28.B66   1996
  650. 1—dc20   96–3454

Printed in the United States of America
1 2 3 4 5 6 7 8 9 0 QF 3 2 1 0 9 8 7 6

Foreword

My mission in life has been to be a conveyor of simple truths. It is for that reason that I'm pleased to be able to introduce the Briefcase Books series, which seeks to provide simple, practical, and direct answers to the most common problems managers face on a daily basis.

It has been my experience that in the field of business common sense is not common practice. So it is refreshing to find a series of books that glorifies common sense in dealing with people in the workplace.

Take the skill of listening. We all know that it is important to listen, yet how many of us actually do it well? I suggest it would be rare to find one in a hundred managers who is truly a good listener. Most people focus on what they are going to say next when someone else is talking. They would seldom if ever think to check what they thought they heard to make sure it is accurate. And they seldom acknowledge or attempt to deal with emotions when they occur in speaking with someone at work. These are basic errors in the use of this basic skill. And regardless of how much education or experience you have, you should know how to listen.

But how much training have you had on the topic of listening? Have you ever had a course on the topic? Have you ever discussed with others how you could listen better with greater comprehension and respect? Probably not. Even though this fundamental interpersonal skill could cripple the most talented individual if he or she is not good at it.

Fortunately, listening is just one of the fundamental skills singled out for its own volume in the Briefcase Books series. Others include books on making presentations, negotiating, problem solving, and handling stress, to name just a few.

The Briefcase Book series focuses on those basic skills that managers must master to excel at work. Whether you are new to managing or are a seasoned manager, you'll find these books of value in obtaining useful insights and fundamental knowledge you can use for your entire career.

Ken Blanchard
Co-author
The One Minute Manager

Acknowledgments

A book like this did not appear magically at your favorite bookstore, but was the result of a number of people who helped me complete my priority: a finished book on priority management. At the top of the list, thanks go to my encouraging and insightful editors, Jeffrey Krames, Robert Nelson, and Patrick Muller; also to my word processing coordinator, Kathleen Radford, who helped me make the deadline; to Pam and Bill Corcoran, who discussed my original idea and gave me new insights into priority management; to my students at Hesser College and my seminar attendees, who supported the book fully; but most of all to my wife, Janet, who put up with my 7-day-a-week work schedule to finish this book.

Preface

Congratulations on the purchase of *Managing Your Priorities from Start to Success*. Studying the tips and techniques it contains will teach you one of the most valuable skills you will ever need: how to get what you want out of life.

This book will not only help you in your job or career, but in all areas of your life. It provides the tools you need to become a priority manager. A priority manager sets goals and sees them through from start to success. A priority manager achieves the things he or she sets out to do. Sound simple? It can be if you know how to go about it. But, as anyone who has ever set out to do something and failed will tell you, it isn't always as easy.

Consistent success in managing your priorities requires that you master the techniques for defining and carrying out your goals. Any skill you learn but fail to use becomes rusty and eventually useless. As you read this book, put the tips, techniques, skills, ideas, and strategies to work. Review them regularly. As one success follows another, you will develop a new philosophy and attitude about yourself and your ability to get things done by priority management. Things that you once only dreamed about will now seem within your grasp.

In my college courses and seminars over the last 25 years, I frequently ask the question "What quality or activity is most important to success?" The most common answers include time management, the ability to focus on positive thinking, working with people, a winning attitude, self-confidence, and organizational skills. None of these answers are completely wrong, yet none of them are

entirely correct, either. The trick is to combine these quali-
ties and match them to the objective you are trying to
achieve. This book will show you how to do just that.

Success is the result of choosing your priorities and directing your activities to meet them on a daily basis. The
strategies and techniques outlined in the following pages
set the foundation for success, but they cannot guarantee
it. Nothing and nobody can do that for you. While success
can be facilitated by effective planning, ultimately it must
come from within. It starts with desire and requires drive,
determination, intelligence, dedication, help, and, occasionally, luck. This book will teach you how—the responsibility to act on what you learn is yours. You and you alone
must decide whether or not achieving your goals will be
worth the effort required. You and you alone are responsible for your future.

Are you satisfied with your life as it is, or are there still a
few things you would like to achieve? If you believe everything in your life is just fine and you're satisfied with the
status quo, then set this book back on the shelf or return it
and get your money back. It's not for you.

If, on the other hand, you still have unfulfilled goals,
read on. It's time to take your life in your own hands and
lead it where you want to go. Decide right now: you are
going to plant your foot on the path to success by setting
challenging, achievable priorities. You will never regret it!
Simply buying this book shows that you are serious. You
have already taken the first—and hardest—step. You have
established a priority and are beginning to take the necessary actions to bring it to successful completion. Let's get
started. There is no time to lose and a great deal to gain.

Contents

Chapter One

What is a Priority Manager?

DEFINING A PRIORITY

Goal: 1) An object or end that one strives to attain: aim. 2) the line or place at which a race, trip, etc. is ended.
Priority: 1) The fact or condition of being prior; precedence in time, order, importance, etc. 2) (a) a right to precedence over other things in obtaining, buying, or doing something (b) and order granting this, as in an emergency. 3) something given prior attention.

Simply put, a priority is a goal that has precedence over other goals. A priority can be personal or work related (or both), simple or multifaceted, easy to achieve or very hard, or any combination of the above. Regardless of its specific attributes, every priority has one common characteristic: it is more important than any other goal or set of goals. It is what one aims for, what one strives to achieve. It is that circumstance which, when achieved, will bring the greatest reward and the most pure form of happiness.

This chapter and those that follow will show you how to identify your personal priorities and offer suggestions and recommendations for achieving them. First, though, it is important to understand where you are headed. Above I have given a single definition for something as vast and varied as the population of our planet. However, there are very possibly more priorites than there are people. And just as priorities share some common characteristics, so too do the people who are able to achieve them—the priority managers.

Knowing what a priority is and being able to achieve it are two very different things. In my years of research on priority mangagement, I have found that certain character- istics lend themselves to success while others are harbin- gers of failure. For example, very rarely will a person achieve a goal if he or she approaches it with a negative at- titude. A negative attitude saps strength, energy, and en- thusiasm and acts as a hindrance and a self-imposed obsta- cle. With a negative attitude, there is no point to beginning because you have already doomed yourself to failure. Take a minute to examine your own attitude. Is your mindset positive? If not, now is the time to fine-tune it so that it en- ables you rather than holds you back.

On the other hand, I have also found certain character- sistcs that are common in people who are able to achieve their priorities. For example, priority managers

- Are self-reliant
- Are aware of both their power and their limitations
- Are patient when necessary
- Have a a clear goal in mind
- Are creative
- Have the support of the people around them
- Recognize opportunities
- Know who they are and where they want to go

Successful people know that the responsibility for their priorities rests squarely on their own shoulders. Turning the priority over to others on the job or at home will not work. You and you alone must manage the priorities in your life. You and you alone will reap the rewards of suc- cess or the consequences of failure. If you want to succeed, stand up and take control. If you don't care, then follow the lead of someone else or ask someone else to do it for you. When you fail, you can always make up some good excuses. Although cliché, the saying is true: "If you want something done right, you have to do it yourself."

Know Your Limitations

Knowing your limitations is important for a couple of different reasons. First, it provides a system of checks and balances for the ego. I, for one, would truly love to be a professional singer. This is not a priority for me, however, because, as anyone who as ever heard me sing will tell you, it is simply not realistic. I am not gifted in that particular area, so I don't waste time that could be spent more productively trying to achieve that goal. I am not suggesting giving up because something is difficult; I am simply stating that by knowing my limitations I focus my energies on realistic priorities.

Knowing your limitations is also important because it frees you to ask for the help you need to accomplish a priority. For example, Pamela works in the accounting office, and her priority is to develop a sales and customer service report for her department. Since she knows very little about sales or customer service, she will need help from these departments to accomplish her priority.

Your power lies in your education, your experience in the field, your skills, and your ability to use the resources available to you.

Use Work-and-Wait Techniques

Just as the mighty oak does not grow to its towering height overnight, reaching success takes time and patience. A billion-dollar bank in New England needed to consolidate its operations so it could better serve customers while increasing revenues. The manager of operations hired an outside consultant, and they worked side by side for one full year until the consolidation was completed.

One of their techniques was to appoint 50 people to various positions within the bank and then meet regularly with them to discuss issues such as reducing waste, keeping morale up, and improving service while increasing revenue. The project took months to complete, but it uncovered many costly expenses, such as multiple newsletter and magazine subscriptions and free coffee to employees. (The cups alone added up to $400,000 a year!) Now, two years later, operating expenses are down and productivity is up. Because they did not expect to see results overnight, the bank directors had the patience to see their priority through to success.

Write Your Own Mission Statement

Writing your own mission statement means stating your priority in a few sentences that detail the commitments you must make. You will learn how to monitor your commitments regularly, to push harder, and to direct your energies in the most promising direction. Good priority management means starting smoothly but moving your priority beyond the obstacles—all the way to a successful conclusion. It means reviewing the mission statement regularly, even reciting it to emphasize its meaning.

The mission statement is your contract with yourself to accomplish an important priority. For example, Joan, who is from Mississippi, wanted to get into the field of robotics. She knew that opportunities existed on the East Coast, primarily in Massachusetts. She wrote the following mission statement to help her achieve her goal.

Mission Statement

To obtain a job in the robotics field and to learn all the latest processes, applications, and benefits of this field. My lifelong priority will be to become a manager or vice president of my company and work on projects serving customers worldwide. I expect obstacles and problems along the way, but I am willing to start at the beginning level and work my way to the top.

Joan moved to Massachusetts and applied to every company working in the field of robotics. After a year, she finally received an entry-level job. She reads her priority statement daily, and through hard work and a willingness to take on extra projects, she expects to get a supervisor's position working with European customers within the next year. Reading the mission statement forces Joan to complete the daily and weekly priorities that will help her reach her lifetime priority.

I work closely with a high-tech company that developed a companywide priority to implement and run a quality control program. It not only developed a powerful mission statement but trained all of its employees in the quality leadership program—at a very high cost to the company. Priorities are not inexpensive; they cost both money and time. Just as a company must develop products that help make a profit, a priority manager must choose priorities that will improve his or her company in today's globally competitive business environment.

Be Creative

Successful priority managers review their skills and strategies regularly and aren't afraid to change their approach to meet their objectives. Janice, a computer sales representative, recently started publishing a newsletter to keep her customers updated on new products and services. The newsletter included examples of how customers are using her products to increase productivity in their operations. For instance, a recent issue included an article about a service company that developed software systems to track the productivity of each service technician: the profit and loss of each call, the calls for the week, and the calls for the month. The newsletter also invites both current and potential customers to attend free seminars where Janice fully demonstrates her products and services.

I recently stopped in a pizza shop while on a trip in Vermont. While I was waiting for the pizza, I talked with the shop owner about Vermont weather and about his business. During the conversation, I found out that the owner only worked in the shop six months a year, from October to March, and worked as a golf professional during the spring and summer months. His business partner travelled in the winter and worked the shop during the summer. Both partners received paychecks all year long. These two men are successful because they were willing to look creatively at their skills, talents, and interests and were able to design a working situation they fully enjoy.

In order to succeed with your priorities, you must be willing to adapt and change. When life hands you a lemon, make lemonade. In other words, be prepared for the unexpected and think "outside the lines" for creative solutions.

Build Support for Your Priorities

A priority will fail unless you first take it seriously and let people know how important it is for the you, the company, or the organization. While you alone are responsible for your priority, it can be helpful to enlist the aid of friends or co-workers—as long as you alone remain in control. Priority managers are salespeople; they sell their priorities to others from start to finish. Promote your priority so that it becomes a priority for others as well. Explain to employees how cost-cutting measures in the production department will result in higher profits for the organization and increase their chances for raises and career success. Remember, the only way to get support for your priority is to openly discuss it with others.

Recognize Opportunities

If I were to assign to you a writing or research project for a course such as accounting, personnel management, marketing, or business law, I would present the idea that you, as the priority manager, need to consider dual purposes; for example, completing the assigned work for the course and then using the material and research to start a business or to write an article for a trade magazine. You have full control over your priority. Your success will depend on your ability to look at your opportunities and your personal situation in a creative way. Accomplishing one priority will increase both your skills and your confidence and enable you to accomplish additional priorities.

A number of years ago, while working as an accountant, I wrote an article on time management for a national accounting magazine. I didn't realize it at the time, but this article would lead to other published articles because it helped me to develop the self-confidence I needed to continue to write and hone my skills. Those articles grew into manuals, books, seminars, speeches, and now videos. You can follow a similar path.

Know Yourself

A priority manager knows what his or her goals, ambitions, desires, and dreams are. In my 30 years of working with clients, students, associates, and seminar attendees, I have found that the most successful people in life are not always the brightest, most talented, or most skilled, but those who have a clear understanding of themselves and what they want to do. Priority managers match their own skills, talents, and desires to a carefully selected priority. Take a few minutes to answer the questions in the following exercise to learn more about yourself.

Inventory Exercise

1. What is your present job?
2. What is your level of education? Your specialty?
3. What do you do in your spare time?
4. What books, magazines, and newspapers do you read?
5. What would you like to achieve at work (i.e., salary increase, promotion, more status)?
6. What is your most important accomplishment?
7. What is your strongest dream in life?
8. If you won the lottery today, how would you spend your millions?
9. In what areas of your life would you like to spend more time (i.e., spouse, children, work, hobbies)?
10. What subject(s) did you enjoy in grade school? Why? What subject(s) did you do well in?
11. What are your main interests? Do you spend enough time in these areas?
12. What goals or activities do you think about accomplishing on a daily basis?
13. Do you enjoy working with people or things?
14. Do you like work in which you can influence others?
15. Do you like to assume responsibility at work? Are you willing to assume responsibility for the work, in terms of both quality and quantity, of others?
16. What makes you happy? If you had to describe your dream job, one that utilized all your potential, what would it be?
17. What special awards, recognition, or special commendation have you received?
18. Do you accept criticism well? Do you spend time and energy worrying about whether or not people will like your work?

19. Can you sell yourself and your abilities to your boss or supervisor?
20. Do you keep up with the latest developments in your job and career field (magazines, newspapers, seminars, tapes, and so on)?
21. Do you think about the possibilities of successful outcomes in your projects or assignments? Are you a negative or a positive thinker?
22. Do you see yourself as just another employee or as a partner in your company, helping it to make profits and reach its goals?
23. Do you find yourself doing boring, routine things at work? Would you like to look at your assignments as unique?
24. Do you find yourself doing things for others? Do you take the time and effort to do things for yourself?
25. How have you changed during the last five years? Ten years? (Look over old letters or recall past conversations.)
26. What changes do you feel you should make in order to reach your priorities?
27. What action will you take to make these changes? What is your time frame for these changes?

SELF-SUMMARY

Now that you've taken inventory, the next step is to write a short description of yourself. One attendee of a priority seminar described herself as curious, humorous, musical, creative, youthful, persistent, a people person, an article writer, a networker, a marathon runner, and a class-A storyteller. Your view of yourself may be quite different from others' views of you. Don't let this deter you. Focus on writing an accurate description for your own use.

Self-Summary

_____

_____

_____

_____

CHOOSING YOUR PRIORITIES

Now that you know yourself a little better, you can match your interests and skills to appropriate priorities.

Priorities May Relate to Hobbies or Interests

When considering work-related priorities, never rule out your hobbies and interests outside the workplace. For example, Tom, an accounting manager, is interested in Model T Fords. He wants to be elected president of his local Model T Ford club so he can get both administrative and public speaking experience. Kathy, an insurance claims supervisor, wants to become a vice president of the insurance company she works for. She has also always wanted to learn to play golf. Realizing that playing golf can help her to expand her networking activities, she has made learning the game one of her priorities.

Know and Share Your Organization's Priorities

Every company wants to succeed in today's competitive business world. Priority managers know that teamwork is crucial to success. Learn the core values of your company or organization and then set your priorities so that they work for the good of all. Numerous consultants have published much research on the reasons why companies succeed and earn profits during competitive times. One of the most important causes of success is hardworking employees whose individual priorities contribute to those of the company.

Even if you work in a smaller company or organization, realize that you are part of an important team and, in that capacity, you might be required to set up priorities that will help your company profit and succeed in the future.

Consider Only Worthy Priorities

Your priorities should be personally meaningful. Sonja is a supervisor of the traffic department of a publishing company, a job that has taught her a great deal about all of the company's departments. Her lifetime priority is to become president of this or another publishing company, something she will work towards accomplishing by setting 1-, 5-, and 10-year goals.

Gail was not a good student in high school. She spent nearly all her time playing sports and socializing with her friends rather than on her studies. Her grades were poor, as were her prospects for college. Gail knew that her high school work was not representative of her intelligence or of her ability to set and reach future goals. Her first step was to enroll in night classes at the community college in order to establish a track record that would qualify her for a four-year college. Because she wanted to go into the communications field, she took a number of classes to build up her writing skills. After a year, she was accepted by a four-year college and is now working for a large advertising agency.

YOU DESERVE SUCCESS

As a unique person with special skills, talents, and abilities, you deserve to choose your own priorities in life. Yet so often others feel they have a right to choose our priorities for us. For example, I recently asked my friend Gus what field his son, who was entering college, wanted to study. Gus said, "He wants to be a teacher, but I told him to go into another field; teaching pays too little, and college is too expensive to just teach." Taken aback, I told Gus that his son should go into the field he wants, and that he has the right to choose his own career.

In the realm of priorities, this kind of behavior is a common obstacle. Many people, including family members, may try to steer you in directions they think are right for you. As a priority manager, you may listen to their opinions and ideas, but you must choose the priority you feel is right.

Many priority seekers try hard but never become priority managers because they hold themselves back from going the extra mile. They become too satisfied with the assistant's job; they settle for the teaching job rather than going for the dean's job; they take the safe, easy job rather than raise their sights and their priorities for the top job.

You are the owner of your career. To get the maximum results from your efforts, meaningful priorities are essential. Would you like to be a supervisor, manager, district manager, national manager, or vice president of your company? Choose a priority that will utilize your skills, talents, and abilities. Remember, your career is really a business; you receive pay for your time, effort, and skills. When you earn $30,000 a year on average for 40 years, you earn $1,200,000.00. If you set workable priorities, your lifetime income could be well over a million dollars.

Now that you've thought about new ways to look at your priorities, fill in the wish list below with the things you would most like to do in your life. (You will be using this list in Chapter 2.)

Priority Wish List

Example: Become a supervisor

1. _Spiritual - Be at peace because of trust in God_
2. _family - Love and respect_
3. _Career - Become a manager_
4. _Black belt in Tai Kwon Do_
5. _Financial freedom_
6. _____
7. _____
8. _____
9. _____
10. _____

SUMMARY

A priority is a goal that has precedence over other goals. A priority can be personal, work-related, or both. It may in fact be the most important thing in your life. Proper priority management allows you to achieve anything you want. Successful priority managers take full responsibility for their priorities, know their power and limitations, are patient, creative, willing to accept assistance, and in touch with themselves and their goals. In order to achieve *your* priorities, start by taking the time to evaluate yourself. What do you love? What makes you happy? Where do you see yourself at various points down the road? Once you have sorted these things out, make a list of what you dream of accomplishing. Aim high. You must believe that you not only can achieve the priority, but that you deserve to succeed.

Chapter Two

Ranking Your Priorities

Now that you've arranged your priorities, it's time for you to choose the one priority that will bring you the most rewards. The first step in this process is to rank the priorities on your list.

There is a difference between priority managers and priority seekers. Many eager-to-succeed priority seekers simply make a huge list of priorities, fully expecting to successfully complete them on schedule. Other priority seekers start so many different priorities they lose track of them, blindly trying to finish some of them—any of them—without taking the necessary time and effort to identify the most important ones.

The ranking you assign your priority is directly related to its reward or payoff. The higher the level of the priority, the more return on investment you expect. For a salesperson, closing sufficient orders to keep the job is a high priority. A medium priority is completing administrative work. A low priority is redecorating the office.

THE REAL TEST

The process of ranking your priorities is an individual one. You, and you alone, must determine what you want. Don't make the mistake of comparing your process with the process or success of others. There will always be some people ahead of you and some people behind you. You are unique; your priorities must reflect your uniqueness.

Your expectations, and your action or game plan, must be realistic. Essential to successful priority selection, therefore, is the REAL test. Too often, priority seekers initially appear to be priority managers, but during the action stage—where the real work is done—they fail to implement the steps necessary to succeed.

Let's look at the REAL test in relation to ranking your priorities. As you examine the priorities wish list you completed in Chapter 1, use the following four qualifications to help you narrow down the list: *Realistic, Easy, Ability,* and *Love.*

Realistic priorities are the building blocks of success. You might want to be the vice president in charge of advertising for your company, but you might need to first accomplish other, more realistic priorities to reach the level where you would be considered for this position. Or you might want to become the top golfer at your country club, but reaching this priority will require committing to other priorities first. Realistic priorities are usually small and relatively easy to handle and exhibit results fairly soon. Achieving success—even on a small scale—will motivate you to set other realistic priorities.

Easy-to-implement priorities give you an opportunity to see immediate positive results. For example, Christine, a graphic artist with a service company, wants to become a supervisor in the graphic arts department. Christine can quickly become her own priority manager by taking management courses as well as learning more about the graphics and computerized services her company offers their customers worldwide.

Focus on priorities you can begin today and keep working hard to reach them. As your priorities become reality, you can go on to bigger and better ones.

Ability also counts in the priorities game. The more ability you have in a particular area, the better your chances to reach the winner's circle. For example, Brandy, a real estate analyst for an investment company, wants to become the supervisor of the training and development department of her organization. Because Brandy studied communications in college and spent years teaching English on the high school level, she possesses the necessary skills and abilities. In order for her to accomplish her priority, she has to find as many opportunities as possible to make presentations to the decision makers within her organization in order to showcase her communication and teaching skills.

Love your priority. If you choose a priority you really enjoy, your chances of success improve greatly. For example, Dave, a supervisor of food operations for a national fast-food chain, has been in the field since he was 15 and would rather be in this business than any other. His priority is to move into upper management in his organization by informing his supervisor of his ambitious plans.

Andrew, a credit analyst for a video manufacturer, wants to become a chief financial officer with his company within five years. Andrew knows he has to gain experience in other areas of finance outside of credit in order to gather the knowledge necessary for the CFO position. But this is no problem, as Andrew enjoys finance and has worked with money all his life. His genuine love of the subject give him the energy and enthusiasm needed to take night classes. Rather than dreading the extra work on top of his day job, he looks forward to the class and enjoys the challenge. He is currently at the head of his class and is right on track to gain the experience he needs to accomplish his priority.

Now it's your turn. Which priorities on your wish list can pass the REAL test? On the line to the left, write down the priorities and check those criteria of the REAL test it meets.

Priority	Realistic	Easy	Ability	Love
_____	_____	_____	_____	_____
_____	_____	_____	_____	_____
_____	_____	_____	_____	_____
_____	_____	_____	_____	_____
_____	_____	_____	_____	_____
_____	_____	_____	_____	_____
_____	_____	_____	_____	_____
_____	_____	_____	_____	_____
_____	_____	_____	_____	_____

Now that you have completed the REAL test, go back and learn from what you have just done. Which priorities are you closest to achieving? Which do you most love? Which will require serious work to accomplish? This exercise should bring you a better understanding of where you stand in relation to your priorities.

I am not suggesting that if you lack the ability right now to accomplish one of your priorities, you should give up. The REAL test doesn't tell you what you can or cannot accomplish, but simply where you stand in relation to the goals you have set for yourself.

CHOOSE YOUR NUMBER-ONE PRIORITY

Successful priority managers learn to handle their priorities over the weeks, months, and years. Focusing on one priority at a time allows you to put your full time and energy into its successful completion. In the space below, write down the priority which scored highest on the REAL test. If more than one satisfied all criteria, choose one that you love the most, is easiest-to-start, and so on.

You are going to become the master of this single priority. You will pursue it from the mental stage, where you contemplate and make your plans, to the physical stage, where you take the necessary action to complete it.

It's a good idea at first to choose a fairly easy priority, so you can see results fairly quickly. Once you've strengthened your priority management skills, you'll be able to tackle the large, longer-term projects. This principle was highlighted during a quality leadership process developed at a high-tech company I recently worked with. Employees attended a four-month course on quality leadership, and after eight weeks, they separated the class into groups of five employees each and asked them to find a problem in the company to fix, to set up a solution, and to get the solution signed off by the instructor and the manager of the department. The final step was a presentation of the solution by all five members to other company employees, including management. The most difficult part of the process was choosing a project that each member of the group would accept. Our instructor, Ron, said, "Choose a project that is fairly straightforward, one that has a solution; try to avoid projects that are too complex in the beginning. In other words, try not to solve world hunger at the Adams company."

SUMMARY

You've now ranked your priorities by subjecting them to the REAL test. You know that to accomplish your priority, it must be *Realistic* and *Easy-to-Start*. It should make use of your *Abilities* and be something you *Love* to do. You've narrowed your options to one *attainable* goal. I will next discuss how to attain that number one priority by setting up a custom-made strategy.

Chapter Three

Getting It Done: Reaching Your Priorities

In Chapter 2, you selected your number one priority. Now you will devise a plan to help you reach it. Priority managers know the value of creating a strategy for achieving their priorities. You will need to examine what it will take to attain yours. As one successful priority manager said, "Looking at what you need to do will help you take the necessary action to get it done."

Winning the priority game involves competition, within your organization and with yourself. Where will you find the time in your hectic schedule to work on your priority? How will you get key people behind it? How will you get the necessary resources—machinery, computers, and data? These are some of the important questions you must answer in order to be a successful priority manager.

SELECT A STRATEGY

Priorities are won or lost largely based on personal strategy you develop for your priority. A mere review of how others once succeeded in achieving a similar priority will not work today: You must be willing to try new techniques while continuing to use those that are still effective. Liven up your approach; do things differently if you need to. Be willing to add an extra dimension to your strategy.

Eileen, a sales manager with a Massachusetts computer company, set a priority of increasing sales by 10 percent next year. Eileen's strategy is to work closely with all of her high-volume customers and find out from them how her salespeople are doing and what changes are needed to increase sales of products and services. Her strategy is a win-win approach—not only will she increase sales in the short term, but, by strengthening her relationship with her customers, she will increase sales in the long term as well. The actions comprising Eileen's strategy are listed below.

Eileen's Strategy

Work Closely with Top Customers and Sales Staff

Actions

- Select the 10 highest-volume customers.
- Talk with the salesperson(s) dealing with the top 10 customers.
- Meet with customers regularly, along with their regular salesperson.
- Invite customers to visit our company to see new products and services.
- Run a seminar on making sales to large companies.
- Determine why some salespeople get large orders and others just get promises.
- Hire a motivational speaker.
- Talk with other sales managers in competing fields.
- Set up a contest for the top three salespeople.
- Informally ask salespeople about their accounts; for example, "How is the Acme account going these days? Did they buy those 100 PCs?"
- Keep telling the team they can reach their priority.

- Say "Thanks" and "Good job" on a regular basis.
- Spend time on these actions every day.
- Write letters to all new and existing customers thanking them for their business.
- Review this list regularly to see which items are working.

In the space below, list your strategy and the actions you will need to take to implement it. You may first want to review Chapter 1. What special talents do you have that could help you make your strategy work? For example, if your chief skill is working with people, your strategy might include getting others involved in your priority. On the other hand, if you enjoy working on your computer and developing new software applications, consider how you can use this talent in achieving your priority.

Priority Strategy and Actions

Strategy

Actions

-
-
-
-
-
-
-
-
-
-
-
-

MAKE YOUR PRIORITY MANAGEABLE

How do you eat an elephant? One piece at a time. Many priorities cannot be accomplished all at once. Rather than focusing on the priority as a whole, then, you need to break it up into a series of smaller steps.

Dyann, a sales representative for a large leasing and financial organization, works out of the Philadelphia area and is under pressure to increase her sales for next year. In order to do that, *Dyann must find new customers.* After identifying potential customers in the hospital and health services field, she determined that her priority would be to focus her sales efforts on this emerging market.

To be successful, Dyann must learn more about this new customer group. How do they purchase products and services? What are their primary considerations before making a purchase? Who makes the final decisions? Customer and product knowledge will be important if she is going to reach her priority. And while working hard to reach the hospital and health care customers, she will also have to keep her existing customers. She will need to develop action steps to support each strategy.

An effective way to look at the priority a piece at a time is to make a to-do list.

Dyann's To-Do List

- Identify new customers in the health care field.
- Read one new trade journal per month to target prospects.
- Read one new book per month on successful selling.
- Schedule appointments with new customers.
- Interview each new prospect about their needs. Identify the decision maker.
- Target specific products and services to quote.
- Follow-up the quotation.
- Ask for the order.

When I discuss this technique of using a to-do list in my priority seminar, some attendees feel their lists are already too full. If you feel this way, take some time to review how you presently use your most important resource; time. Do you have time available, even a small amount—15 minutes, 30 minutes, or an hour per week or even per month— to spend on your priority? If not, reevaluate how you spend your time. Where are you spending time on something not as important for you? (A helpful hint: Kill your television set!)

USE YOUR RESOURCES

Successful priority managers learn early on that there are resources available to them in the form of people and information. Be willing to seek them out. Some resources are free, such as libraries. Others, such as databases and global Internet, need to be purchased but are often available through your company or organization.

Let those around you—your spouse, your boss, your business associates—know about your priority and how important it is to you. People will help you when you ask for their help and are committed.

KNOW YOUR PRIORITY TIMETABLE

Estimate how long it's going to take you to complete your priority. Try to give yourself enough time to do a good job. Some priorities will take six months; others will take a year or even more. In the spaces below, write in deadlines for completion of your priorities. Estimate their completion dates to the best of your ability. Make sure your deadlines are attainable and, whatever else you do, stay with them!

Priority	*Deadline for Completion*
_____	_____
_____	_____
_____	_____

BE DISCIPLINED

If you wait until you have time to work on your strategy, there's a good chance you won't get much done. Instead, you need to discipline yourself so that you work on your strategy every day. Stan, an accountant, wants to advance his career by learning to speak more effectively in public. His top priority this year is to get the training and experience necessary to do so. His strategy is to join a local speaker's club, which will force him to speak at each weekly meeting, and then to take every available speaking opportunity at work or at his local service club.

Because Stan realized that the best speakers not only speak well but also present solid information to their listeners, he began looking for newspaper and magazine articles that would provide substance for his speeches. He also began reading and taping speeches given by top speakers all over the country to get new ideas on how to effectively present information. He now listens to tapes of effective speeches while driving to work. Not a day goes by that he does not do some kind of work on his strategy.

AVOID EXCUSES

In the words of Minnesota Fats, "The only thing a loser needs is an excuse to lose."

Excuses are priority blockers; the energy used to summon them up will sap your energy and your desire to get other things done. Excuses will also earn you the reputation of a poor performer and an unreliable worker. Remember, the priority is yours—*you* have the most to gain or lose from its success or failure. A good excuse might help you save face, but you can't fool the only person that really matters. You will always know whether or not you could have done a better job in trying to reach your priority. Some of the excuses priority wasters use to give themselves a facade of credibility appear below.

Common Excuses

- My sales were good for the first month; the recession hurt me.
- I'm only a few days late; I'll put in for another extension.
- I'll do it as soon as I finish a few little things around here.
- I was going to call yesterday, but other things came up.
- I expected it to be done by now. I'll get back to you.
- I gave the job to Sam; I assumed he'd finish it on time.
- I never get any help around here.

SUMMARY

You need to develop your own strategy to achieve your priority. Write up your lists and formulate an action plan. Remember to make your priority manageable. Above all, remember that your strategy is a work in progress and needs daily attention. If you miss a deadline, revise it; don't get discouraged, and above all, don't give up. Good priority managers adjust to changing forces of business or personal circumstances.

In the next chapter, we'll discuss overcoming obstacles.

Chapter Four

Overcoming Obstacles

Every worthwhile priority will face obstacles. Successful priority managers handle these obstacles and get right back on track. An obstacle is merely a flat tire on your three-week vacation. You don't need to end the vacation and go home; you just need to replace the flat with your spare and then get the flat repaired.

Successful priority managers develop options. They not only have a Plan A but a Plan B and C to use when a strategy is no longer working or when the results are not as strong as they'd like them to be. Determining the best plans requires looking ahead and listing all the possible obstacles you can imagine.

ANTICIPATE OBSTACLES

What can potentially slow you down in the attainment of your priority? People? Methods? Machines? Systems? Your boss? Yourself? Review your achievements over the past few years. What were your main obstacles?

Rachel knew that one of the largest obstacles to getting her strategy successfully started would be her boss in the main office, who could potentially bog her down by asking her to retrieve information that was easily available on the network. Rachel's strategy was to inform her boss that he could get the information faster on the network.

By reviewing the most common obstacles, you will be in a better position to handle them as you encounter them. Below, list the possible obstacles to your priority and then list the possible solutions.

Obstacles   *Possible Solutions*

_____   _____

_____   _____

_____   _____

_____   _____

_____   _____

_____   _____

SUCCESSFUL CONFRONTATION

Try not to overreact to the obstacles in your path and try not to read anything into them until you've had time to examine them fully. For example, Sondra's top priority is to automate the production department of a toy company. She is working closely with Gretchen, an expert on software for production systems who has worked with the employees in the company for over five years.

Recently, Sondra and Gretchen have been arguing about automation methods, and Gretchen has been spending large blocks of her time on other clerical work and projects for her boss—activities outside her priority. Sondra is concerned with the fact that her priority is going to take longer than she'd originally planned without Gretchen's full interest and effort.

As a priority manager, Sondra can do two things: (1) she can pay no attention to the problem and hope Gretchen will start on her priority and finish it successfully and on schedule, or (2) she can confront Gretchen directly and work out a new strategy and to-do list to insure the timely and successful completion of the priority.

Let's listen to the conversation between Sondra and Gretchen.

Sondra:

Gretchen, do you have a few minutes to discuss our automated toy-making project?

Gretchen:

By all means.

Sondra:

When we agreed on the project, we talked about having the software done by October first. It's now the middle of September, and we haven't even scheduled a meeting to discuss the results.

Gretchen:

I'm sorry about the delay. I've been pulled away from the project by my boss for the past two weeks. I'll have the software program together by Friday. Would you like to schedule a meeting for Monday?

Sondra:

That's fine. Is 10 o'clock alright?

Gretchen:

Fine. See you then.

Successful priority managers know that firm control is necessary to get others keyed into their priorities. Some of those involved in your priority in various ways will test you by delaying their work, just waiting to get your reaction. Once you confront them directly and in a positive manner as Sondra did with Gretchen, they will usually be happy to put your priority on their to-do list or to at least give it the attention it deserves.

If you're not comfortable confronting others, you need to develop your confrontation skills. Timing is important. The longer you delay the confrontation, the more difficult it will be. You also need to realize that confrontation in this context is not synonymous with aggression. The point of a confrontation is to get the problem out in the open and find creative ways of solving it, not to antagonize your associates.

Bill is the accounts receivable supervisor for a large service and presentation company. His number-one priority is to collect the over-90-day accounts to add to his company's cash flow. To add visibility to his priority as well as educate others about it, Bill designated his priority "Operation 90."

Bill recently noticed that Linda, an associate working on this priority with him, was not focusing and that as a result the priority not only wasn't gaining the momentum he'd expected but was in fact falling behind schedule. Rather than ignoring the problem, Bill confronted Linda in order to get some necessary feedback.

Bill:

Linda, can I talk to you for a few minutes about Operation 90?

Linda:

Sure. I think it's really going to help our cash flow management around here.

Bill:

I'm happy to hear you say that. How are your over-90 accounts going these days? Is there anything I can help you with?

Linda:

No, I don't think so. I just need to find the time to do all the things I need to do.

Bill:

You're right about time being scarce around here, Linda. However, the accounting department is meeting next Friday to discuss Operation 90. It would really help to have your accounts in by then.

Linda:

I'll look over my accounts and try to get all in by Wednesday.

Bill:

Thanks for your help, Linda. I'll see you at the meeting next week.

Notice what took place here. Bill, as manager of the priority, knew that making it work would require the cooperation of others. He took the positive approach, confronting Linda in a professional, nonthreatening manner that got the importance of the priority across.

HANDLING COMPLAINTS

Complaints go with the territory. Your priority is going to affect others, and there will always be those who will voice their displeasure at the fact that your priority is throwing them off their daily routine.

One technique in handling complaints is to tell the complainer the purpose of the priority and the possible rewards. For example, "Yes, Alice, there will be extra paperwork, but this information might help us earn a profit, and that could lead to raises and promotions."

Sometimes, complaints can be a valuable source of information especially when more than one person complains about the same product or service. These complaints could provide the basis for researching a solution. The successful priority manager sorts through complaints and pays only minimal attention to normal complaints, but takes action on the more serious ones. Many successful companies take customer complaints very seriously and act on them swiftly, even giving refunds when appropriate.

Examples of "normal" and "serious" complaints follow. As you will see, the normal complaints are counterproductive, draining energies that could be better focused on completing the priority. The "serious" complaints, on the other hand, point out failures in the current system or obstacles that are impeding the successful completion of priorities. Although normal complaints are a hindrance, serious complaints can facilitate the completion of your priority. The trick is to distinguish between the two.

Normal complaints

- My cubicle is too small.
- *I* shouldn't have to do this if *he* doesn't.
- This extra work means I don't have time to take a full hour for lunch on Thursdays.
- I don't want to go to the seminar this week because it takes too long to get there.
- I hate having to wear a tie to work everyday.

Serious complaints

- I spend too much time traveling on my job. I could sell more if I travelled less.
- I am the one who does all the hands-on work for this project, but upper management never even asks for my ideas on how to get it done.
- I spend too much time filling out the same information on different forms. If we combined the forms, I would have more time to work on the priority.
- It takes too long to get the things I need to complete the priority because of the bureaucracy in this office.
- Most of my work is with the people on the second floor. I could be much more productive if I didn't have to walk down three flights of stairs every time I needed to talk with someone or get some information.

DEVELOP ALTERNATIVES

Blaming others when you run into obstacles to your priority is not effective priority management. A more effective technique is to have an alternative plan when a strategy doesn't work. Darnell, a supervisor with a telemarketing company, is looking for an opportunity to get into management but blames his boss for not giving him the opportunity. Darnell is hurting his chances to succeed because he has taken his mind off his work and is focusing more on his obstacles rather than on ways to handle them.

Suzy's number one priority is to run a marathon. In order to accomplish this, she needs to spend at least an hour training every day. Recently, her boss threw a major obstacle into her priority path when he asked her to stay an extra hour late each night in order to work on the year-end report. Suzy likes and needs her job, so she had to comply with her boss's request. She didn't, however, let this obstacle interfere with her number-one priority. She realized that working an extra hour every night would take away her training time, so she developed plan B: Rather than letting her boss kill her priority, Suzy now gets up at 5:30 every morning so she can train for an hour before work. This way, she gets her training in and still stays late to help her boss with the year-end report. It isn't easy for her, but the love she feels for her priority gives her the energy and enthusiasm to do it.

INVOLVE YOUR PRIORITY TEAM

When your priority hits an obstacle, you might get so upset that you're unable to see the strategies needed to solve the problem. This is when support and feedback

FIGURE 4–1
Storyboarding

Obstacle	Possible Solution
Employees are not working on my Acme account priority.	Hold a meeting with them.
	Send out a memo.
	Cancel the Christmas party.
	Talk with key people in the department
	Review your original strategies.
	Remind employees of rewards. Tell salespeople why you need their efforts to succeed.

from other members of your priority team are important. Some priority managers meet with their teams regularly—once every month or two; others meet only when enough obstacles warrant it. Be sure to fully inform your team about each obstacle so they can offer their most useful suggestions. Tell your team you need their valuable input and thank them for their suggestions. Some priority managers list their team's answers on a sheet of paper or on the blackboard, a technique known as *storyboarding* (see Figure 4–1).

Write down every idea, even if it sounds silly. A "silly" idea might be the springboard for developing a workable solution. Your job is to choose the very best suggestions and test them. Review your notes regularly to make sure you are using all of the ideas, strategies, and insights available.

REWARD YOUR SUCCESSES

Your success depends upon your feeling good about yourself and your priorities. Work on solving your problems, but also reward yourself for your successes. Priority seekers maintain their seeker status by focusing only on setbacks and obstacles and never celebrating or reinforcing their successes. Look for the positive things that happen daily and give you the added momentum to get things done. Take yourself out to dinner, buy yourself a gift, call someone and discuss your success. Celebrating and enjoying those little successes will help you keep your priorities on track.

TURN OBSTACLES INTO CHALLENGES

Behind every difficulty lies an excellent opportunity to push yourself closer to your priority finish line. Look at every obstacle as a kind of challenge.

Randy is a video sales representative in California, and he just won a contest on selling a new product in his video line. Prior to winning the contest, Randy was way behind the other sales representatives, but by working extra hours and calling on more customers he won the contest. Since he won the contest, Randy is selling more than ever because he enjoys telling his customers about the benefits of his new products and his success as a sales leader.

People like to be with and do business with a winner. As one priority manager from Baltimore said, "I try to deal with setbacks simply as temporary delays in my well-organized priority process."

LEARN FROM DEFEAT

Every priority has a life of its own. You can work with it, reshape it, adjust it fully, and reestablish a new strategy to reach it, but for one reason or another you still might fall short.

Take the example of Coleen, a computer specialist who took a temporary job with a men's clothing store to set up an inventory system for them. Coleen learned that the inventory system was very important to the company because it was used to get the credit line from their bank. Starting at the beginning of June, she set the priority with her boss to automate the full system by September 1st. Coleen worked very closely with all departments, gathering information and working late into the evening and on weekends. By late August, Coleen brought her results to her boss, and after a review they decided more work was needed to finish the priority. However, Coleen's contract would expire before she could complete the task. Coleen was angry that she could not finish her priority, but she considered her work successful because of the experience she gained.

Remember, if you learn from defeat, you haven't really been beaten. Coleen was able to bring the experience she gained from this project to her next, where she used her experience to create a more realistic action plan and time frame to carry out her next priority.

MAKE THE MOST OF CHANGE

Change is an inevitable part of life. As we approach the year 2000, changes in business will become more and more far-reaching, especially as a result of organizational changes such as downsizing, reengineering, rightsizing, and consolidation of assets and operations.

Many people have an aversion to change and secretly hope that if they ignore it, it will just go away. But the fact is that change offers tremendous opportunities for success. Priority managers know how to view change positively, adapt to it, and gain maximum benefits from it.

In order to fully deal with change, you must fully examine it. Below are some important questions to ask yourself about a particular change.

Questions About Change

1. How is this change affecting me?
2. What are the positive aspects of this change?
3. What are the negative aspects of this change?
4. How have others handled this change?
5. What resources do I have within me to deal with this change, (i.e., computer skills, negotiating skills, etc.)
6. What can I do to learn more about this change? What is needed to deal with it?
7. How can I use this change to reach my priorities?

TAKE CHARGE OF CHANGE

Jim owns a restaurant and coffee shop in Pennsylvania. When his business began to slow down and problems began to multiply, he started thinking about all the possible excuses he would offer when people confronted him about the situation. Using his energy and creative resources in this way, however, only slowed him down further. Finally, he decided to take action and create new ways to promote and market his business—his number one priority.

Jim knew that to get customers to return day after day would require regular discounts, motivating ads, and, most importantly, a focus on customer service. He began to make a point of asking each customer if she or he was satisfied with the meal. If there was a problem, he gave the customer a gift certificate to use on another visit. He began to notice that not only were new customers coming in but regular customers began to stay longer and spend more money.

Jim replaced his excuses with success because he took the steps necessary to deal with the negative changes in his business.

A customer service representative for a large computer software company, Tara's number-one priority was to become manager. She poured herself into her work, going the extra mile to make certain her customers received the best service; working overtime, including many weekends; and always looking for new ways to improve herself and her department.

When Tara heard rumors that her company was experiencing financial problems, she passed them off as just that, rumors. But on her way to work one morning, she heard on the radio that her company had just filed for bankruptcy. Tara began to see her promise to herself as her number-one priority.

At a departmentwide meeting, Tara learned that this was not the end but in fact could possibly mean renewal for the company. Since the bankruptcy was a Chapter 11 filing, the court would give the company a chance to continue operating the business, try to establish a profitable record over the next few months, and eventually emerge from bankruptcy.

Tara decided to deal with this change immediately. She spoke to other people in her department about the filing as well as to people in other companies that had survived bankruptcy. In addition, she reassured her customers, who, while surprised at the news, were very supportive. Tara decided to roll with the punches and worked even harder in her job to help her company beat this bankruptcy filing. She even had a letter published in the company newsletter that voiced her optimism about how the company could succeed if everyone worked together.

A full 18 months later, Tara's company came out of bankruptcy. She now expects to become the manager of her department.

SUMMARY

You will have greater success as a priority manager if you anticipate obstacles before they happen. That way, you'll always have alternative plans ready to counteract delays. As a successful priority manager, you must sometimes confront situations before they become problems.

Positive, professional confrontation, with plenty of constructive feedback, will bring desired results.

Remember, obstacles are opportunities in disguise and the only mistake is the one you didn't learn from. Plan for change, embrace it, and use it to your advantage.

Chapter Five

Keeping Your Priority in Sight

No one starts at the top. Many successful people started at the bottom, but they had one intangible ingredient that was extremely valuable to them: a vision of what they wanted to be tomorrow and the desire and motivation to keep working to reach it.

THE VISION STATEMENT

Do you want to become the best financial advisor, retail executive, or insurance representative? Do you want to become the best software sales representative or compensation and benefits manager in your field? Write a few sentences to describe your vision. To do this, you will have to consider your talents, resources, and special skills. Below are a few sample vision statements.

Video store manager trainee
I'd like to be a retailer with district management responsibilities for 12 to 24 video stores nationwide, utilizing my people management skills to train and develop my team into the best in the chain. I want to be happy and to make others around me happy.

Computer operator for financial company:
I would like to use my intelligence, my communication ability, and my understanding of computers to start my own computer and software applications company geared to small business.

Professor and author of self-help books:
My vision is to live with all the enthusiasm, vigor, and spirit possible, while teaching, writing, and sharing my philosophy of life with others, hopefully helping them to achieve more in their lives.

Recent college graduate:
My vision is a career in biotechnology and, with the help of my organizational ability, a balanced life that also permits marriage and children.

Now it's your turn. In the space below, write your vision statement. You may want to review Chapters 1 and 2 first to refresh your memory about your skills, interests, and talents.

_____

_____

_____

_____

SHARING THE VISION

You can't achieve your vision all by yourself. A vision also needs the support of others—a warm, loving environment that will sustain it. Once you've written your vision statement, your job will be to let others know about it and how working with you to achieve it can result in mutual satisfaction and rewards.

Jordans, a furniture company in New England, is one of the most successful in the country because it continually focuses on satisfying the needs of customers. Their employees all know its philosophy: pricing, products, and professional sales personnel must all combine to satisfy the customers. The company regularly monitors priorities and helps the staff to reach them. This sharing of the vision has its paybacks in corporate performance.

Your Personal "Vision Day"

Successful priority managers know that constantly dealing with daily issues and concerns leaves little time to stoke the fires of a strong vision. You need to break your regular routine and carve out time to pursue and embrace your vision. Use the time in your personal "vision day" (or half a day or even several hours) to examine what you must do now and in the future to achieve your priority.

For example, you might buy a book on individual investing in order to get your personal finances in order. Or you might have lunch with a former classmate who was just promoted to vice president and discuss the strategies and techniques she uses.

During your personal "vision day," avoid the temptation to think about your worries, the obstacles, and setbacks we discussed in the previous chapter. Enjoy yourself! Nurture your priority in positive, meaningful, and rewarding ways.

VISUALIZING SUCCESS

You know what needs to be done. You know what action you must take to turn things around. You are the manager in your life. But most people try to do too many things.

They do a little of this, a little of that, but they skip over the carefully selected priorities that could give their life special meaning.

If you neglect your priorities, they begin to gather dust and lose their true meaning. A participant asked about this during a seminar on priorities replied, "After giving it careful analysis, I really believe I sabotaged my success by being angry. Angry with myself and angry with others, especially the people who were able to accomplish priorities similar to mine." His comments are important because they illustrate the importance of having a quiet confidence within yourself—not only about your vision of the future, but about all the necessary steps to success.

Visualization can help you achieve this confidence.

Your priority is the light in the darkness, the clearing in a valley of fog. But you must *believe* you can accomplish your priority, your vision, before you can carry it off in the real world. Successful priority managers not only see themselves achieving their vision but also achieving—step-by-step—the priorities that will get them there.

Surgeons use a step-by-step visualization technique before operating, going over each of the steps in the operation in their mind's eye. When they run into trouble with one of the steps, they begin again. You can do the same. When preparing to give a speech at the local business association, for example, visualize yourself being introduced, introducing your speech, and then moving on to the heart of it.

Take time to learn the visualization process and practice it daily—in your car, while waiting between appointments, and during coffee breaks and any other free time available to you.

Even though you may not be able to actually work towards your priority every day, you can at least give it visualization time.

Visualization Can Be Partly Negative

Some people motivate themselves by pondering the negatives that can result if their priority fails. A salesperson visualizes the pink slip she'll receive when she fails to make the sales quota; a student sees himself not graduating because he fails a course; a computer specialist imagines losing a promotion for turning in an assignment late and still incomplete.

There is nothing harmful about looking at the potential results of a priority suffering setbacks—*as long as you take the time to refocus and look at positive outcomes as well.*

Visualization Takes Time and Effort

Training is not enough; education is not enough; a privileged background is not enough. To become all you can be also requires that you make the necessary effort and take the necessary time—5 minutes here and 10 minutes there—to visualize your priority. The 15 minutes on the bus or subway each day or the 30 minutes on the freeway can be excellent opportunities to view your successful progress in the theater of your mind.

Begin with a few minutes a day. Eventually, visualization will become habitual; you will be able to comfortably increase the time you spend visualizing and thus improve your prospects for success.

SUMMARY

Achieving any priority requires a full awareness of exactly what it is you are trying to achieve and the steps that you will have to take to get there. First, identify your priority by writing it down. This vision statement will help clarify your objectives as well as the resources you bring with you to help you achieve it. Don't be afraid to share this vision with others, for help will only bring you to success more quickly. It is important to periodically step back and take a look at the big picture rather than just the details, so take a personal vision day. And finally, use the process of visualization to keep yourself on track and bring your priority to success.

Chapter Six

Time Management

One of the most important questions I ask my priority seminar attendees is simply this: Do you use the clock as your friend and ally? Many attendees confess that they begin each day with a sense of optimism and a commitment to giving a large measure of time to their number one priority. But, as the day unfolds, they give little, if any, actual time to it. Successful priority managers stand out from the crowd because they take advantage of the precious gift of time. Remember, being successful doesn't make you manage your time well. Managing your time well makes you successful.

TAKE THE INITIATIVE

Nothing is more important to successful time management than the ability to start a job even if you only have a few minutes to devote to it. Starting the task breaks the ice, increases your confidence, and directs the momentum towards a successful completion. Some priority managers write up a list of every step necessary to complete the priority. Then they choose the quickest, easiest job to get the process in motion. This is similar to putting your foot in the water at the pool before you dive in.

LEARN THE VALUE OF TIME

You have worked hard to develop a good reputation at work; people respect you, and your boss asks your opinion on a regular basis. Your time is valuable; don't let others waste it.

Murray works for small businesspeople all over the state and is so committed, dedicated, and involved with their problems that he doesn't even bill them for his consulting services. Murray's number one priority is to help his clients become successful. One month, when he couldn't make a rent payment, he decided to check his billing records for the previous month. Sure enough, he hadn't billed anyone for the entire month. He decided that in order to stay in business he would have to bill customers $50 per hour for each consulting job. Once he began regularly billing his clients, his volume of work actually increased because his clients realized he put a value on his time.

The time you spend on your priority is so important that you have to consider the return you will receive on it. For example, say you're doing a year-end report for your boss on the ABC account. You want to show your boss how much ABC spent with your company and the profits you earned with them. Since you are the account manager with the ABC company, this report is important to your career and future earnings. If you get a $5,000 raise from the positive report for the company, and you spend 10 hours of overtime to do it, the value of each hour is $500. This is an excellent return on investment.

Priority managers know the value of time and develop a consciousness of it. When they find themselves wasting time or spending it on trivial or low-payoff activities, they quickly turn to high-payoff activities, such as the ABC account report. The most important thought to keep in mind is that doing things right is not as important as doing the

FIGURE 6–1
Tips and Strategies for Working Productively

- Why am I doing this?
- What is the goal?
- Why will I succeed?
- Is what I am doing at this minute moving me toward my objective?
- What will happen if I choose not to do it?
- What am I doing that doesn't really need to be done?
- What am I doing that could be done by someone else?
- What am I doing that could be done more efficiently?
- What do I do that wastes other's time?
- If I don't have time to do it right, do I have time to do it wrong?

---

right things. Figure 6–1 gives some important questions to ask yourself when determining how productively you are spending your time.

Profit from Your Prime Time

Prime time is that part of the day during which you are the most productive, most creative, and most ingenious. It is very important to ascertain when your prime time occurs—defend it ruthlessly. Use this period to get your most important and difficult tasks done. Conversely, recognize "dead" time. Schedule meetings, phone calls, and mundane duties during those periods.

Ann is a morning person; she gets her best work done before noon. Frederick gets into gear in the evening, and so he does many of his projects late at night and into the early morning. Patricia, also a morning person, gets up at six A.M. and plans her priorities for the day. She lays the groundwork for her day by making a list of the things she wants to do. You possess a unique biological rhythm. Once you've assessed it, you can put your time to its best use.

In addition to time of day, prime time might also refer to a time in your life. Rob is a mechanical engineer. During his twenties, he worked with customers. Now, in his thirties, he is in the research and development department, working on new products. Rob is maximizing his experience and interests to get the best return on his investment time. Time managers mesh their specific priorities with their use of time, reserving their prime time for their most important pursuits.

BECOMING A BETTER TIME MANAGER

Those who best manage time make the best priority managers because they know how to get the most important work done. In my seminars, I have found that the top time managers have a common characteristic: They plan their daily activities, and then they follow their plan.

Karol, a supervisor, claims she finally started to reach her priorities when she began spending an hour each morning during the commute to the office planning the most important activities for the day. She jots down notes; tape-records ideas; and visualizes how she will approach, execute, and direct her activities for that day. Karol views each day as the only day, even the last day, of her life. She made a statement in the seminar that summed up her philosophy on time: "There are two days I don't worry about: yesterday, which is gone, and tomorrow, which may not even arrive. I realize today is mine." Priority managers know that the real wealth is time.

Figure 6–2 is Karol's to-do list. A to-do list to help you set up a plan to organize your day follows it. Jot down a list of 7 to 10 things you would like to accomplish tomorrow at work.

FIGURE 6–2
Karol's To-Do List

1. Research ABC account for staff meeting.
2. Finish report on discounts for boss.
3. Work on inventory report.
4. Write outline for sales seminar.
5. Pick out office furniture.
6. Set up appointment with XYZ Company for demonstration.
7. Choose office wallpaper.
8. Make follow-up calls to make sure packages arrived on time.
9. Read mail and answer phone messages.

To-Do List

1. _____

2. _____

3. _____

4. _____

5. _____

6. _____

7. _____

8. _____

9. _____

10. _____

FIGURE 6–3
Prioritization Utility

---

1. Important AND Urgent

Priority one jobs are yours alone and you must plan these into your day. They consist of the most important steps to completing your priority. They generally must be done well and immediately.

2. Important NOT Urgent

Importance outweighs urgency. Important things are those which only you can do or which can advance you toward your life goals.

3. Urgent NOT Important

Priority three jobs and paperwork are delegated if possible or assigned a small time slot and routinized.

4. Neither Important NOR Urgent

Priority four paperwork gets the least (if any) attention, and priority four jobs are put in a separate bin that you only look at in your spare time or when you have completed all other to-do tasks. As the least important, they get the least time and attention.

Successful time managers know that the next step is to prioritize the items on their lists. Figure 6–3 outlines the process of prioritization utility. This simple process will help you determine which items need to be dealt with immediately, which can be delegated, and which can be put off until a later date.

Figure 6–4 illustrates how Karol ranked the items on her to-do list, utilizing the priority utility standard.

FIGURE 6–4
Karol's Ranking of Items on To-Do List

Rank	Item
#1	Finish report on discounts for boss.
#1	Research ABC account for staff meeting.
#2	Work on inventory report.
#2	Write outline for sales seminar.
#4	Pick out office furniture
#2	Set up appointment with XYZ Company for demonstration.
#4	Choose office wallpaper.
#3	Make follow-up calls to make sure packages arrived on time.
#3	Read mail and answer phone messages.

Below, you can rank the 7 to 10 items on your to-do list.

Ranking of Items on Your To-Do List

Rank	Item
___	_____
___	_____
___	_____
___	_____
___	_____
___	_____
___	_____
___	_____
___	_____

FIGURE 6–5
Karol's Revised To-Do List

---

1. Finish report on discounts for boss.
2. Research ABC account for staff meeting.
3. Work on inventory report.
4. Write outline for sales seminar.
5. Set up appointment with XYZ Company for demonstration.
6. Read mail and answer phone messages.
7. Make follow-up calls to make sure packages arrived on time.
8. Pick out office furniture.
9. Choose office wallpaper.

Finally, you are ready to revise your to-do list. In Figure 6–5, notice that Karol moved her #1 items to the top of the list, followed by the #2 items, and finally the #3 and #4 items.

Below is space for your own revised to-do list.

Your Revised To-Do List

1.

2.

3.

4.

5.

6.

7.

8.

9.

10.

PUTTING YOUR PLAN INTO PRACTICE: THE TIME LOG

Now that you have a properly organized list of things to do tomorrow, it is time to test yourself. Tomorrow at work, keep a time log for yourself (see Figure 6–6). For each 15-minute interval, log in the task that you were working on at that particular time. (Important: don't wait until the end of the day to do this: take just one minute every quarter hour to jot down your notes. That way, you won't forget.) Then, in the column labeled "Priority Number," assign the task a number using the priority utilization system outlined earlier. Most likely, not everything you do tomorrow will be on your to-do list. Unexpected interruptions will throw your plan off.

You will be amazed by what you learn about yourself. Did you work on the inventory report for your boss or did you spend your time answering questions for your friend in customer service? The time log is the only way to truly assess whether or not you are putting the strategies and techniques to work. If you aren't honest with yourself about how you are spending your time, this exercise will be futile.

At the end of the day, review and assess how you have spent your time. In the column labeled "Comments on the Effective Use of Time," state how you performed in your time use for the day. Look for general trends. What activities could have been delegated? What activities did you work on that are neither important nor urgent? Did you get all the important and urgent items accomplished first? How many items on your log were on your to-do list? When you have filled out the log, make some general comments and then grade yourself for the day. Figure 6–7 is an example of a completed section of the time log for your reference.

FIGURE 6–6
Time Log

Time	Task	Priority Number	Comments on Effective Use of Time
Date _____ Name _____			
9:00–9:15	_____	_____	_____
9:15–9:30	_____	_____	_____
9:30–9:45	_____	_____	_____
9:45–10:00	_____	_____	_____
10:00–10:15	_____	_____	_____
10:15–10:30	_____	_____	_____
10:30–10:45	_____	_____	_____
10:45–11:00	_____	_____	_____
11:00–11:15	_____	_____	_____
11:15–11:30	_____	_____	_____
11:30–11:45	_____	_____	_____
11:45–12:00	_____	_____	_____
12:00–12:15	_____	_____	_____
12:15–12:30	_____	_____	_____
12:30–12:45	_____	_____	_____

1:00–1:15   _____   _____ _____

1:15–1:30   _____   _____ _____

1:30–1:45   _____   _____ _____

1:45–2:00   _____   _____ _____

2:00–2:15   _____   _____ _____

2:15–2:30   _____   _____ _____

2:30–2:45   _____   _____ _____

2:45–3:00   _____   _____ _____

3:00–3:15   _____   _____ _____

3:15–3:30   _____   _____ _____

3:30–3:45   _____   _____ _____

3:45–4:00   _____   _____ _____

4:00–4:15   _____   _____ _____

4:15–4:30   _____   _____ _____

4:30–4:45   _____   _____ _____

4:45–5:00   _____   _____ _____

General Review and Comments _____

_____

Grade _____

_____

FIGURE 6–7
Illustration—Time Log

Date <u>March 13</u>   Name <u>Sonia Ford</u>

Time	Task	Priority Number	Comments on Effective Use of Time
9:00 - 9:15	5 yr Plan	1	Good
9:15 - 9:30	"	1	"
9:30 - 9:45	"	1	"
9:45 - 10:00	Filing	3	Poor Use
10:00 - 10:15	Coffee	3	" "
10:15 - 10:30	5 yr Plan	1	Good
10:30 - 10:45	"	1	"
10:45 - 11:00	"	1	"

Keep in mind that this is not a one-day exercise. Do it three days in a row. Wait a month and then do it another three days. Wait two more months and then do it again. In fact, continue throughout your life to assess how well you have mastered the skill of time management. Did your grade improve from month to month? If you find your grade starting to slip, it might be time to review this chapter. What general trends have you found? Where is your time being wasted? What things consistently take too long? The rest of the chapter outlines some tips and strategies for dealing with and beating interruptions and time traps.

DEALING WITH INTERRUPTIONS

Just because you choose your priority carefully and begin it immediately in the morning does not guarantee that nothing will get in the way of your progress. The phone rings. Frank in shipping and receiving has a question about yesterday's receiving reports. Monica in corporate sales wants your future projections on the sales in your department. Deal with these minor interruptions, then be sure to return to the priority you set for yourself at the beginning of the day. In cases where you cannot deal with the situation quickly, inform the person who has interrupted you that you will get back to him or her later.

Interruptions abound from the moment you wake in the morning until you fall asleep at night. You must learn to manage them, or the balance will reverse itself—the interruptions will manage *you*. The difference between finishing an important job or project on time or being forced to make an excuse for your delay will depend on how you manage yourself and your interruptions and make each day count. For example, the average interruption takes from six to nine minutes. It then takes another two to three minutes to get back to where you were before it occurred. From this logic, five interruptions can waste a whole hour of your valuable time.

There are many kinds of daily interruptions, not all of them caused by other people. Below are descriptions of the most common kinds and ways to handle them.

Telephone Interruptions

Paul is a single father with four children under 14. His children's phone calls to him at work were becoming more frequent and longer. In order to fulfill his work priorities, Paul had to develop a strategy for dealing with these costly, and mostly unnecessary, interruptions. He eliminated the problem by calling home at a set time each day to talk to his children. He also told his children and his secretary that he would only accept emergency calls or short calls of less than two minutes each. A successful priority manager cannot stop working every time the phone rings.

FIGURE 6–8
Tips and Strategies for Telephone Interruptions

- Keep calls short.
- Begin the conversation by saying "I only have two minutes." This can always be extended.
- Stand during the call.
- Start by announcing your goals for the call.
- Don't put your feet up.
- If interrupted by a call during a task, write down what you were thinking before answering the call; you will then know where you left off.
- Have something in mind that you're waiting to get to next.
- Don't always answer.
- The person who makes the call has the psychological "right" to terminate it. It's better to ring back so you have that right.
- When you've accomplished what you needed, end the call (hang up if you must).
- Group your outgoing calls together, i.e., just before lunch and at 5:00 P.M.

Figure 6–8 lists useful strategies successful priority managers use to deal with telephone interruptions.

As technology advances and people have greater access to each other at all times, these tips will become even more useful.

In-Basket Interruptions

Greg started his number-one priority, but, after working on it for only 30 minutes, he started going through the pile of papers in his in-basket. Some of them were quite interesting. One thing led to another, the number-one priority was left behind, and Greg fell further and further behind in his work.

It's important to stay ahead of your cleaning to avoid the stacked-desk interruption.

FIGURE 6–9
Tips and Strategies for Dealing with Paperwork

- Avoid procrastination.
- Only read something if you'll be fired for not reading it.
- Keep your desk clear and focus on only one thing at a time.
- Clutter is death—only have on your desk the items that you are dealing with.
- When in doubt, throw it out.
- Touch each piece of paper only once—don't pick it up unless you intend to finish it at that particular time.
- A good filing system is essential.
- Most correspondence can be answered on the letter or memo it was sent on.

Figure 6–9 lists some strategies successful priority managers use to deal with paperwork and avoid the stacked-desk interruption. It is important to remember that these strategies apply to routine paperwork such as interoffice memos and junk mail rather than reading and research necessary to stay abreast of your particular field.

Delegate!

A common complaint in numerous offices in the 1990s is, "I'm exhausted; I know I'm taking on too much work." Delegating work is a necessary skill for the successful priority manager. Let's see how Janet, the claims manager of a large insurance company, delegates work to her assistant manager.

Janet:
Please sit down, Steve; I want to review the invoice sent to the ACME account.

Steve:
What's wrong? I double-checked it before it was mailed.

FIGURE 6–10
Tips and Strategies for Delegating Work

- You can accomplish a lot more with help.
- Delegate wherever possible, but do not abdicate—you are ultimately responsible.
- Grant authority.
- Require responsibility and accountability.
- Treat your people well.
- People rise to the challenge: you should delegate "until they complain."
- Give objectives, not procedures.
- Explain why the task is important.
- Make sure that the instructions for delegated tasks are complete, clear,and have been fully understood.
- Jot down assigned tasks so that you can keep track of them.

Janet:

There's nothing wrong with the invoice, but their accountant called me and wanted more details so they can process it more quickly.

Steve:

What information do they need?

Janet:

The full serial numbers, all part numbers, and the shipping invoice need to be attached to the invoice for this account. I'd like you to take care of that please.

Steve:

Sure, and I'll make sure it's done in the future so you won't have to deal with any more calls.

Janet:

Thanks, Steve.

Figure 6–10 provides some tips that successful priority managers use when delegating. Remember, delegation does not mean dumping!

DEALING WITH TIME TRAPS

Just as interruptions can stand in the way of accomplishing your priorities on time, so too can the way you do things. If someone were to calculate the cumulative amount of time wasted every day by the U.S. workforce, the number would be staggering. Time is our most precious commodity, yet every day people everywhere throw hours and hours out the window. A major difference between people who accomplish the things they set out to do and those who fail is the way they spend their time. The following paragraphs describe some of the most common ways in which time is lost and strategies for how to avoid these traps.

Don't Follow the Crowd

The cafeteria is jammed at noon. The highways and subways are filled to capacity during the morning and evening rush hours. A journey that should take only 20 minutes ends up taking more than an hour because everybody else is travelling at the same time. People stand in interminable lines at the bank at noon and on Fridays. Not only is standing in line incredibly frustrating, it is a complete waste of time. In order to avoid this trap, why not vary your schedule? For example, many companies allow flextime now, meaning that—to a limited degree—you can set your own work hours. Even though you prefer to sleep in, why not switch your hours from 8:30–5:30 to 6:30–3:30 to avoid the daily traffic jams? Perhaps you should take your lunch at 11:00 or 1:30 to avoid the lines at restaurants.

If varying your schedule isn't an option, then ask yourself, "What productive work could I be doing while I wait?" Getting some reading done? Listening to instructional tapes in the car? Perhaps brainstorming ideas into a small tape recorder? All these suggestions turn wasted time into time that will bring you closer to accomplishing your priority.

Be Practical

Another common way in which time is lost is through doing things the hard way when there are easier, faster, and more productive methods available. For example, when Dave, a sales representative with a large distribution company, completed a sale, he had to send one report to the warehouse so the product got shipped to the customer, another report to the local office so the customer got billed, and a third report to the national branch so his year-to-date figures could be tracked for commissions and payroll. Filling out all three forms was tedious and time consuming, so he decided to combine all three reports. What used to take 15 minutes now takes only five. Considering he was making about five sales a day, Dave has saved himself about 10 minutes filling out forms for each sale. He now has an extra hour each day to focus on selling, and he has become the leading sales rep in the branch.

Look over some of the things you do on a regular basis, such as writing letters, daily reports, weekly or monthly communications, or other procedures. What if you stopped doing them? What if you altered them slightly? It is important to step back and review the processes for your job, because simple changes can save countless hours of work.

Technology can also play an important role in streamlining processes and saving time. Computers are becoming ubiquitous and, as technology improves, they are helping people do things faster and better. In fact, today's technology is enabling many people to work out of their homes. With computers, fax machines, and telephones at their houses, much of today's workforce has become more productive than ever. Not only do they save time once lost commuting, but by working from home they avoid the interruptions and distractions common to offices.

SUMMARY

The most successful priority managers are people who make the most of their time. Time is our most precious commodity, yet a staggering number of hours are wasted everyday because people don't know how to manage it properly. When trying to reach your priority, jump right in and get to work. The first step is always the hardest. Your time is valuable so make the most of it. Doing things right is not as important as doing the right things. Schedule your day so you know what you should be working on. Do the most difficult things on your list at the time of the day when you are most productive. Do the least important things during your downtime. Test yourself on how well you manage your time by creating a time log. Follow this exercise daily, monthly and annually to review your progress and identify the areas in which you need to improve. Most importantly, spend the bulk of your time on the things that will help you accomplish your priorities.

Chapter Seven

The Importance of Relationships and Information

To succeed in the priorities game, you must not only demand your own best efforts, but also permit everyone involved with your priority to share ownership in it.

GET EVERYONE INVOLVED

Successful priority managers are willing to ask for help from others and to continuously sell the benefits of their priority. Take the example of Ned, a financial business owner. His priority is to increase sales by 10 percent across the board. He runs contests to help his managers increase their performance goals, with prizes that include trips to other countries, bonuses, extra time off, and company cars.

Merely setting a goal, however, is not enough; you have to be willing to encourage everyone within the company to strive for this goal as well. Ned takes the time to train and work with any manager who needs extra help, and he sets up regular meetings with the managers so they can share their ideas about how to make the 10 percent priority a reality.

You can also give your team members pep talks, similar to those I give my students, especially the ones who aren't grasping the material quickly enough. I tell them, "If you can dream it, you can do it" and encourage them not to give up on themselves. Below are several examples of statements you can use to involve and motivate others.

Statements for Involving and Motivating Others

- Thanks for your help; this will help me finish priority number one.
- Priority number two is running behind schedule. I could use your help. Here's all the information on it.
- I realize that all of you have been putting in an inordinate amount of time and effort to complete this project on time. I can't give you the day off, but I want to take everyone to lunch to show my appreciation.
- Your help and ideas on the last project was invaluable and I let my boss know it. We were wondering if we could get your help on this next priority.

QUALITY COMMUNICATION COUNTS

You will succeed in the priorities game only when people feel comfortable with you. Artificial friendliness will not work; people know when you care about them enough to communicate frankly with them. People want to feel involved and be acknowledged for their contributions. Today's workforce is the most diverse in history. Words differ in meaning between departments, organizations, and cultures—in fact, 50 percent of all attempted communication is lost or misinterpreted.

Look the other person straight in the eye. Nothing is more important in communicating your message than looking squarely at the other person and being aware of her or his reaction to your message. If you look away or down at the floor, the person might think you are trying to hide something or that you're not sure of the message you want to send.

Ask easy questions of the person you're dealing with; this will show you have an interest in his or her ideas. Pay attention to the responses, not only to what is being said but how it's being said. Everyone is important, from the person on the lowest rung to the person on the highest. Know the first name of everyone in the company and use it regularly. This shows that you respect the individual, not his or her position. Remember, this applies to *everyone*, not just the people who hold higher positions or that you work with directly. Sooner or later, positions will change, and no one can ever have enough allies. Something as simple as a "good morning" when passing in the hall can give you an advantage.

Take time to thank all those who helped you achieve a priority, whether verbally or through a companywide memo. People need to be recognized for their work. A simple, sincere show of appreciation will help win support for all future priorities. The point is, simple acts of respect will pay huge dividends in the long run.

LET OTHERS SET THEIR OWN PRIORITIES

You will attain your priority when you take the responsibility of tapping into the talents and skills of others on your priority team or within your organization. At a recent seminar, Margaret, a successful priority manager, said "Genius is the gold in the mine; talent is the miner who works to bring it out." The people around you will implement their own priorities. Your job is to become the supervisor in the goldmine, to direct the miners and extract the gold.

Christopher is a sales manager for a consulting business. His eight sales representatives set their own monthly priorities for sales levels. Christopher tries to get them to stretch themselves to reach even higher levels of success rather than get bogged down in a comfort zone and settle for the easy priority.

FIGURE 7–1
Monthly Sales Priority

Name	Carol Neville	
Priority	$100,000.00	
A.	*Confirmed Sales*	
	Bordensworth Co.	10,000.00
	Smithhurst Co.	15,000.00
	Total confirmed	$25,000.00
B.	*Possibilities for Success*	
	Forwardly Co.	40,000.00
	Eastonville Co.	5,000.00
	Ryanon Co.	2,000.00
	Total possibilities	$47,000.00
C.	*More Challenging Sales*	
	Parrot Co.	12,000.00
	Sarantos Co.	8,500.00
	National Assoc.	3,500.00
	Littleton Corp.	4,000.00
	Total	$28,000.00
	Grand Total	$100,000.00

Figure 7–1 is Christopher's monthly sales priority. During the second week of each month, Christopher and the sales staff get together to go over the customers on his list. Christopher tries to get the possibilities in Section B and C to become confirmed sales, like Bordensworth and Smithhurst in section A. The more challenging sales must be worked and watched closely. Christopher encourages his salespeople to consider their monthly priorities as opportunities to showcase their skills and bring in the sales that the company needs to stay in business. He tries to keep the communications with the salespeople not only upbeat but also full of humor.

Christopher also sponsors sales priority contests awarding as a prize for the top salesperson of the month a dinner for two at the winner's choice of restaurant. If a salesperson loses a sale, he will talk to the sales representative about the reason for the loss and try to replace the loss with other customers. In other words, Christopher forms full partnerships with his people in order to get the results necessary to succeed.

LET OTHERS KNOW YOUR EXPECTATIONS

Much has been written about expressing your appreciation and thanking people for their efforts, not just at the completion of the mission, but during it as well. What about setting limits and letting people know where you stand with them? Many priority managers get better results when they communicate to others around them their expectations for success.

Take, for example, Lorenzo, a foreman with a paper recycling company. The general manager asked him to become the company's safety manager and to set up a safety committee. Lorenzo didn't know anything about safety except the precautions he took on his own job. So he read books on the subject, attended some seminars, and took a first-aid class.

Then he met with his safety committee and laid out its ground rules and goals. He drew up a priority team contract similar to the one in Figure 7–2 and went over it with the team members. The important point he emphasized is that if the team fails, *everyone* fails—and so does the organization.

Lorenzo made it clear that he was always willing to help any team member who needed it. But when a member failed to carry out his or her responsibility, he made sure the team member heard about how the team had been let

FIGURE 7–2
Priority Team Contract

- Our priority has been carefully selected and agreed upon by all.
- If management asks how we're doing, I'll tell them, "Just great."
- If you have a problem or concern, I'll try to help you with it.
- I'll work with you to do whatever is necessary to assure your success in learning the techniques and completing your safety priority.
- I'll be available when you need me.
- If the team fails, we all fail.

---

down by this behavior and stressed that it couldn't happen again in the future. If it did, the team member would be expelled from the committee.

Let people know you have standards—and stick to them.

THE IMPORTANCE OF INFORMATION

In addition to treating co-workers as an important resource, you also need to use other sources of information. The people who reach high-payoff and timely priorities are not just lucky. They possess the most important advantage resource next to effective time management and good relationships: The ability to handle information in a creative and professional manner.

Information may not be readily or easily available, so you need to know how to find it. Having the right information helps you to avoid guessing or estimating when the boss, the organization, or the customer wants you to be precise. Access to the right information gives you an additional, powerful boost over the competition.

Take the example of Edward Johnson, owner of Fidelity Investments. Years ago, he set a priority to make his company the top mutual fund company in the country. He knew that investors needed information in order to make good investment decisions, so he advertised his mutual fund services widely in business and metropolitan newspapers. Johnson offered his customers updated information seven days a week, 24 hours a day, on their investment accounts, including the net asset value, the price per share, and other information customers needed to make their buying and selling decisions.

Because of the way his company used this valuable information, it is now the top mutual fund company in the country. Reaching this priority took a great deal of time and effort, especially from the company's individual fund managers, who worked hard to turn out exceptional results quarter after quarter, year after year. These managers spent countless hours gathering the necessary information on companies and organizations before investing in them.

Where do you get the information to reach your priority? It depends on your priority. Many small businesses use the resources of the research department of the local public library. Research librarians have access to magazines, directories, books, specialized governmental publications, trade associations, newsletters, and the Internet. The government offers a tremendous amount of information, most of it free. Figure 7–3 is a listing of U.S. governmental agencies that publish information. You can receive a catalog of over 200 free and low-cost federal publications of consumer interest by writing to Consumer Information Center, P.O. Box 100, Pueblo, Colorado 81002.

Other sources of information include studies by specialists, consultants who specialize in a specific field, research firms that conduct surveys to determine the reasons for people buying or not buying your product or service, and focus groups—a session of people assembled expressly to look over your products or services and give you their views, both favorable and unfavorable. Cable television,

FIGURE 7–3
U.S. Governmental Agencies

Commodity Futures Trading Commission
Congressional Committee
Consumer Product Safety Commission
Department of Agriculture
Department of Commerce
Department of Defense
Department of Education
Department of Energy
Department of Health and Human Services
Department of Housing and Urban Development
Department of the Interior
Department of Justice
Department of Labor
Department of State
Department of Transportation
Department of Treasury
Department of Veteran Affairs
Environmental Protection Agency
Federal Communications Commission
Food and Drug Administration
Federal Deposit Insurance Corporation
Federal Emergency Management Agency
Federal Financial Institutions Examination Council
Federal Reserve Board
Federal Trade Commission
General Services Administration
Health Care Financing Administration
Interstate Commerce Commission
Internal Revenue Service
Library of Congress
National Aeronautics and Space Administration
National Archives and Records Administration
National Endowment for the Arts
National Endowment for the Humanities
National Institutes of Health
National Institute of Mental Health
Office of Consumer Affairs
Postal Service
Small Business Administration
Smithsonian Institution
Social Security Administration
Selective Service System

with its proliferation of business and educational programs, may also be an important source of information. And the computer revolution has produced databases and on-line subscription services offering an incredible amount of information to businesspeople and professionals.

The Basic Types of Information

All information is either primary or secondary. Primary information is that which you personally collect; for example, the survey you sent to your customers last year that gave you information on their ages, occupations, incomes, and geographic locations, or the results of the focus group you assembled to discuss a new product or service.

Secondary information has been gathered, and probably analyzed, by someone else and is available in the form of books, magazines, reports, videotapes, and so on.

Phyllis, a sales manager for a large insurance company, hired an outside consultant to determine the most effective techniques for helping her company increase its sales during the following year. The consultant, using the primary information method, interviewed hundreds of companies, sales managers, and sales representatives both inside and outside the insurance field. Although this method of information gathering is more expensive than purchasing a book or report that has done the information gathering for you, sometimes you tailor your research to your specific needs and analyze the results yourself, making the expense well worth it.

Inside and Outside Information

Before spending large sums of money on an outside consultant, don't overlook the value of inside information, which is readily available within the departments of your company or organization in the form of sales, expenses, profits, losses, number of employees and suppliers, capital assets, liabilities, and working capital, and other information you can obtain from your own colleagues.

Outside information is the information on competitors and on governmental agencies that pass laws and regulations affecting your business. Other outside information will come from labor unions, the general public, and the stockholders or owners of your organization. The more information you have on and from these sources, the easier it will be to set strategies to successfully work with them.

SUMMARY

No man is an island. No matter what your priority is, your chances of reaching success will be greatly improved by enlisting the aid of all resources available to you. The two best resources are people and information. Enlisting the help of people is not a one-time maneuver but a continual effort to show respect to everyone in your company. There is no more effective motivator than a handshake, a look in the eye, and a sincere "please" or "thank you." Beside co-workers, the next best resource for achieving your priority is information. Successful people know how to creatively access and use information. The computer age is making more information available to more people than ever before.

Chapter Eight

Evaluating Your Priority

Businesses, industries, governmental agencies, and not-for-profit organizations spend a great deal of energy and money evaluating their products, services, employees, and operations. As a consumer, you have probably been asked to fill out an evaluation after dining in a restaurant, having your car serviced, taking a course, applying for a loan, buying a house, or even paying a bill. Such evaluations ask you, "Will you please tell us how we are doing?"

In this chapter, you will be asking yourself this question: How am I doing with my priority right now? The information you gather in answering this question will help you learn about your priority, yourself, and the actions you need to take to reach your own level of success.

WHEN TO EVALUATE

When is the best time to evaluate your priority? A snappy answer to this question would be "every day," but realistically, whenever you feel you need to take a look at it in more detail you should step back and examine whether or not your priority is still truly important.

Just as you know when your car isn't handling the way it should and needs service, you will know when your evaluation needs a tune-up as well. For example, if you find yourself less enthusiastic about carrying out your priority than when you started, it could be a sign that it no longer *is* a priority for you. If so, take the necessary steps to renew enthusiasm. If not, you have just freed up time to complete a true priority.

HOW TO EVALUATE

Some priority managers use the informal evaluation method to evaluate their priority. The immediate group working on the priority meets for coffee or a quick meeting on priority progress and to ask questions such as these:

1. What is going right?
2. What is going poorly?
3. What adjustments can be made?
4. What changes have occurred since the priority was started?
5. How can we take advantage of these changes?
6. What are our strengths/opportunities?
7. What are our weaknesses/threats?

After the meeting, the priority manager can make a list of the ideas and suggestions that were brought up and distribute them to everyone in the group.

But, while groups can be helpful in evaluating a priority, too often the views are far-ranging and therefore not especially helpful. Perhaps a better place to begin is with your general impression of the status of your priority. Do you see any real progress towards its completion? When do you expect to finish it? What is the most damaging element to your progress? People? Resources? Time?

Sometimes it's helpful to go over your daily time log to see the comments you made about your priority during the last few weeks or months. Go through the file on your priority and review materials such as letters and notes.

This general overview can help you spot situations or trends that might need to be corrected.

Write out your general impression of your priority below.

_____

_____

_____

_____

_____

_____

_____

After completing this general impression, you will be in a position to do a more formal, in-depth evaluation of your priority.

WHAT TO EVALUATE

Just as important as knowing _how_ and _when_ is knowing exactly _what_ to evaluate. Think of your evaluation as a measurement in a chemistry experiment. Measuring the wrong things will not only ruin the outcome, it can be dangerous as well. If, on the other hand, you measure the right things at the right times, you know how well you are proceeding toward the desired outcome.

Below are the items that need to be measured closely to bring your priority to a successful conclusion.

Evaluate Your Attitude

Manuel was upset because he felt he was not making the progress he needed to make in order to become human resources manager in his company. He got so upset, in fact, that he began to lose his positive attitude, becoming negative about himself, his associates, and the company. This attitude was counterproductive, of course, since the job to which he aspired involved working well with others. Needless to say, he never became the human resources manager. If he had stepped back and evaluated his attitude, he could have gotten himself back on track to achieve his priority.

Danielle, a management consultant, set a priority to only accept clients who had a problem that she could identify with, had a passion for, and could enjoy helping to solve. At one point, however, she was so unhappy with herself that it bordered on depression. She knew she had not been true to her original priority and her strategies to achieve it. Below is her general evaluation of her priority:

> When I accepted the XYZ account, I told them I would only do their business plans. Now, weeks later, I'm in charge of new store openings all over the country and doing their employee training. I'm not having the fun I expected. I need to make some changes to keep my sanity and my career.

Danielle decided to discuss her situation with the president of the XYZ company and was reassigned so that she could concentrate on writing the company's plans and marketing strategies. She is much happier now because she is doing what she enjoys.

Evaluate Your Energy Expenditure

Priority seekers often know what activities are necessary to win, but fall into the trap of engaging in activities that will not produce the desired results. Susan, a territory manager of a national soup company, set a priority this year to increase new sales by 10 percent. Each quarter, Susan wrote out her general evaluation of her priority's performance, focusing on where she was spending her energy. She found that she had been spending nearly 20 percent of her mental and physical time at work helping Kevin in the production process. While her help was greatly appreciated and obviously benefited the company, it was preventing her from achieving her priority. After the evaluation, she went to Kevin and told him that she was sorry but would not be able to help him in the future to streamline the production process. She then used the available time on increasing her sales. By year end, she had exceeded her priority and new sales were up 13.5 percent. Through evaluating the energy she spent, she was able to recognize where she needed to spend more time if she was going to successfully complete her priority.

Figure 8–1 is a list of activities. In the appropriate columns, indicate how much time you spend on each.

Now that you have evaluated how much energy you spend on some common activities, decide whether or not this is the best way to bring your priority to successful completion. For example, if you are a father whose priority is to spend as much time as possible with your child and you spend a great deal of your at-home time watching television, then something is obviously wrong. Spend your energy in the most effective way possible. If necessary, go back to the time management strategies outlined in Chapter 6. The time log, too, can give you a good indication of where your energy is being spent.

Evaluate Your Stress Management

Your priority evaluation might reveal that your stress level is too high, and this might affect your priority and your health. Examine the reasons for your stress. When do you feel the most stress? How do you relieve it? Some people find that exercise is a good stress reliever.

Stress may be the result of bottling up your emotions. A famous philosopher once asked, "What is a man or woman without emotions?" In your priority process, be willing to get mad, cry, or laugh at yourself. Nature has

FIGURE 8–1
Where Do You Spend Your Energy?

	Little or No Time	Moderate Amount of Time	Large Amount of Time
At Work			
• Talking with customers.	_____	_____	_____
• Doing daily reports for boss.	_____	_____	_____
• Going to unnecessary meetings.	_____	_____	_____
• Writing unnecessary memos.	_____	_____	_____
• Fixing mistakes made by other employees.	_____	_____	_____
• Assisting your assistant.	_____	_____	_____
• Traveling.	_____	_____	_____
• Working on your number one priority.	_____	_____	_____
• Working on your department's activities.	_____	_____	_____
• Working with suppliers.	_____	_____	_____
• Attending seminars and workshops.	_____	_____	_____
• Socializing or making personal phone calls.	_____	_____	_____
• Reading newspapers or magazines.	_____	_____	_____
At Home			
• Watching TV.	_____	_____	_____
• Spending time with family and friends.	_____	_____	_____
• Playing sports.	_____	_____	_____
• Reading.	_____	_____	_____
• Listening to music.	_____	_____	_____
• Taking courses.	_____	_____	_____
• Hobbies.	_____	_____	_____

provided these outlets for you for a reason. Stress managers, people who know that stress is normal in today's world, use techniques to help them deal with whatever comes down the pike. Below are some simple guidelines to help you better handle stress.

Stress Busters
_____

- Believe in yourself fully.
- Learn to laugh at yourself.
- Be high on yourself; you're special just the way you are.
- Take a daily brisk walk; it works wonders.
- Take time to be alone.
- Say no to the things you don't want to do.
- Communicate to others; try to give compliments.
- Do what you enjoy doing.
- Ask for help when you get overloaded.
- Open your life to others.
- Leave room in your to-do list to handle the unexpected.
- Ask for an extension; anything worthwhile in life takes time.
- Choose a hobby that gives you pleasure.
- Expect change; it's part of life.
- Take a deep breath.
- Eat in a quiet place.
- You're part of the human race; don't expect perfection.
- Don't put excessive demands on yourself.
- Take mental vacations to calming, enjoyable, and renewing places.
- Work as part of a team.
- Learn to meditate or pray regularly.
- Permit others to take the credit for worthwhile accomplishments.
- Do a slow dance with today; enjoy it fully.
- Relax; you know how to manage your priorities and your life.

Evaluate Procrastination

Christine wants to become a partner at her public relations company. Her evaluation showed that too many important assignments were being delayed or swept aside, causing her to fall behind schedule. When Christine analyzed the tasks she had put off, she realized they involved dealing with difficult-to-please customers or situations where the customer refused to pay for certain public relations projects. Further analysis revealed that Christine needed to focus on her people skills, the ability to gather the information on each case and to present it fairly.

You will not reach your priorities unless you learn to make the decisions necessary to cut your losses, keep the customer happy, and go back to the work at hand. Delays only hamper your process, deflate your confidence, and force you to keep procrastinating on important tasks. During a priority seminary, Linda summed up her feeling about her approach to problem solving this way: "I learned from my boss to solve each problem as quickly as possible and avoid letting them build up." You can do this, too.

Evaluate your ability to learn from others within your office, department, or organization. Frequently, excellent role models are not adequately consulted by the people who could benefit from them the most: those working close to them.

Evaluate "Perfection"

You must someday realize that, no matter how hard you try, you cannot have everything. Focus on the priority at hand and do your level best to reach it. Don't fall into the trap of chasing perfection so obsessively that you lose track of your priority.

Anthony, an attendee of a priority seminar, said, "I know what I should be doing to reach my priority, but I get too busy with minor details and rechecking the work I already checked; I lose out in the end." Examine the trends in your working style. Do you continuously check others' work along with your own? Can you put this time to better use? If excessive checking is important to you, perhaps you can delegate or hire someone to do it for you.

Evaluate Your Renewal Process

Without renewal, you can become stale, tired, and stuck in a rut rather than utilizing the creative ideas and techniques that will add to your progress and your priority. Go to a seminar, take a class, take some vacation time, read a book, join a club, or visit a museum or art gallery. In short, step back and look at your work, your life, or your priority from a different perspective. See the big picture rather than always focusing on the details. You can accomplish this in a wide variety of ways, from going to work on a Saturday when no one else is there to discussing your priority with a friend or co-worker, thus getting fresh insights or ideas.

SAMPLE PERSONAL PRIORITY EVALUATION

Companies have their own evaluation techniques to help them move into the winner's circle. An example is An-heuser Busch, brewer of Budweiser beer. A 118-year-old company based in St. Louis, it is trying to maintain strong sales in order to retain the title "The King of Beers." Its marketing executives conduct many evaluations to determine how its products are standing up to the competition. Recently, the company changed advertising agencies. They are also considering introducing new brands but will release them only when their evaluations show they can hold their own and will complement the other products within the Anheuser-Busch family.

You must evaluate your priority in the same manner million- and billion-dollar businesses do. You own your business just as they do. You need to take a good, hard look at your business and avoid decisions based on guesses.

Figure 8–2 is an evaluation survey that will help you to learn more about—and reach—your priority, which will ultimately help you reach success.

Once you've completed this evaluation carefully, read through it again. The comments you made will help you deal with both your current priority and future priorities. Analyze what contributed or detracted from your success and make adjustments and corrections.

Leo is a real estate representative for a medium-sized real estate agency. His priority was to learn the selling techniques that would help him land a sales management position. Leo took all the training available at his company, as well as correspondence courses on sales techniques and management. Six months into his priority, he completed his priority evaluation and found that his most difficult area was dealing with others one-on-one. Leo decided he needed more practice role-playing in the sales process and more experience in day-to-day selling situations in order to get the skills he needed for success. Use the evaluation to help get your priority on track and to develop those important skills that will help you succeed.

SHARE YOUR RESULTS WITH OTHERS

Rachel, a transportation worker, completed her priority evaluation and found that she needed to work more evenings and some weekends to complete her priority within the deadline. When she talked it over with her husband, daughter, and son, they jointly decided they could arrange their lives to permit Rachel the time she needed to reach her priority.

Jack, a sales representative with a clothing manufacturer, completed his evaluation and determined that his sales forecasts were so high he just didn't have the physical

FIGURE 8–2
Priority Evaluation

Directions:

Please complete the following evaluation. Your observations will help you to make the best possible decisions about how to reach your goal. Be willing to return to earlier sections of the book to gather information on creating and setting strategies and on monitoring your time and energy.

	Yes	No	Comments
1. Do you feel as strongly about your priority today as you did when you set it?	_____	_____	_____
2. Do you work on, or at least think about, your priority every day?	_____	_____	_____
3. Do you reward yourself for daily or weekly successes?	_____	_____	_____
4. Do you communicate the benefits of your priority to others regularly?	_____	_____	_____
5. Are you using those skills, talents, and abilities shown in your inventory?	_____	_____	_____
6. Do you use the strategies you developed for your priority?	_____	_____	_____
7. Are you using the resources available to you to reach your priority?	_____	_____	_____
8. Are you adhering to your priority deadline?	_____	_____	_____
9. Do you handle complaints and negative comments about your priority well?	_____	_____	_____
10. Do you view setbacks as part of the priority manager's job?	_____	_____	_____
11. Do you take time to visualize your ultimate success daily?	_____	_____	_____

	Yes	No	Comments
12. Do you make excuses when you fail to finish your priorities?	___	___	_____
13. Did any important changes occur since you set your priority?	___	___	_____
14. Do you regularly keep your return on investment in mind?	___	___	_____
15. Are you managing your time so you can reach your priority?	___	___	_____
16. Do you spread yourself too thin and run out of time?	___	___	_____
17. Do you keep your personal obligations and work obligations separated?	___	___	_____
18. Do you plan each day with your number one priority in mind?	___	___	_____
19. Do you review your activities to determine which ones can be shortened, reorganized, or terminated?	___	___	_____
20. Can you hire help, contract for temporary help, or purchase outside contractors to help you?	___	___	_____
21. Can you use your commuting time differently to save time for your number-one priority?	___	___	_____
22. Do you get enough people involved to get the best possible results?	___	___	_____
23. Is your priority important enough to help establish a reputation?	___	___	_____
24. Are you selling your priorities to others regularly?	___	___	_____

	Yes	*No*	*Comments*
25. Are you keeping up with new information that can benefit your priority?	____	____	_____
26. Are you building a network of people who can help you now and in the future?	____	____	_____
27. Are you changing with the needs of the company?	____	____	_____
28. Is your present number-one priority in line with your organization's needs?	____	____	_____
29. Can you reshape your number-one priority to meet the needs of your reorganization?	____	____	_____
30. What have you learned from this priority about yourself, others, and the process itself?	____	____	_____
31. What do you do when you're in a negative mood to get refocused on your priority?	____	____	_____
32. Do you still get excited and dream about reaching your priority?	____	____	_____
33. Do you continue to sharpen your critical thinking skills?	____	____	_____
34. Do you surround yourself with positive people who believe in you and your priority?	____	____	_____
35. What do you want to choose for a future priority?	____	____	_____
36. Did you select a priority that was too ambitious or too easy for you?	____	____	_____
37. What are the most important factors in your success?	____	____	_____
38. Did you have fun in the pursuit of your priority?	____	____	_____

		Yes	No	Comments
39.	Did you ask for help when you needed it?	_____	_____	_____
40.	Did you share your priority with your spouse or significant other?	_____	_____	_____
41.	What relationships were beneficial to the progress of your priority?	_____	_____	_____
42.	What skills do you need to complete your priority?	_____	_____	_____
43.	Did you learn from past mistakes and apply those lessons to future priorities?	_____	_____	_____

resources to reach them. After discussing this at a family meeting, Jack decided to ask his boss for some time off, which his boss was happy to give him. After a week of vacation, Jack came back refreshed and renewed. He used this vacation time to look at his priority in a different light. When he did return, he was ready and willing to get to work on meeting his forecast. Plus, he had some fresh ideas about getting the job done. Discuss your evaluation with the people close to you—with their support and encouragement, you can reach full success together.

Just as it is important to learn from past mistakes, so too it is important to learn from past successes. When something does go right, examine the situation and figure out why it went right and the steps you took to bring about success. If you understand *why* something went right, you can apply those same principles and techniques to future obstacles, thus improving future chances for successful priority completion.

The following questionnaire will help you identify some of the reasons you were successful in the past and how those skills can be applied to current and future priorities.

Priority Success Skills

Why were you successful in the past?

_____

Are you still using these skills today?

     Yes _____   No _____

If no, why not?

_____

What skills are needed to improve your performance?

_____

What are the things you need to finish your priority (i.e., people, time, resources, help from management, etc.)?

_____

Are you willing to ask for them to finish your priority?

     Yes _____   No _____

If no, why not?

_____

Who will you ask to obtain what is necessary to finish your priority?

_____

What is necessary to help you finish your priority? Be as specific as necessary.

_____

SUMMARY

In order to successfully complete your priority, it is important to consistently evaluate your progress. In doing so,
take a look at your attitude, the time and energy you spend
on it, your stress management techniques, and your drive
for perfection. Be sure to periodically step back, look at the
big picture, and renew your enthusiasm for the priority.
Share what you have learned from the evaluation with the
people that are most important to you. Also, examine past
successes and the steps you took that made it successful.
These steps will help you learn about your priority and
yourself and will help pave the way for success in all future priorities.

Chapter Nine

Adjusting Your Priority

Now that you've evaluated your priority, it's time to make the necessary adjustments to it. Your priorities are not cast in stone. You change, and circumstances change. Your job can change. Your organization can—indeed must—change to succeed in the 21st century. Read the changes and stay alive.

Steve is a controller with a company that produces computer hardware. His priority was to develop techniques to help the company earn larger profits. After working on this priority for several months, Steve did an evaluation and found that his company was focusing more on the consulting and business software side of the business and less on the hardware side.

Consequently, Steve decided to change his priority to one with a higher payoff: learning more about consulting and business software accounting procedures. Although Steve changed his priority, he took with him all the information and experience he had gained from working on his initial priority. It's important to recognize that your time and effort is never wasted when it's spent on trying to achieve a priority. When changing priorities, your chief job is to transfer the knowledge and information you gained in one area into the new area. By making this adjustment you exhibit the real-world skills of the priority manager.

Dawn is a maintenance supervisor with a housekeeping department of a large city building. She enjoys her job, and by working hard on her priorities she has continued climbing the ladder to the supervisor's position. Dawn's two biggest challenges, however, were to get along better with the people who worked for her and to motivate them to do higher quality work. She decided she would make these concerns her number one priority.

After working on her priority for a number of months, Dawn saw some important changes: She felt much more comfortable dealing with other people, and she had begun putting into place an excellent technique for evaluating her employees' performance. But after weighing the time and effort going into it, she was still unhappy about her priority. After doing a priority evaluation, she decided that she really wanted to work in the computer selling field, selling small to medium-sized computers. Consequently, she decided to refocus her energies and skills on a new priority—becoming a salesperson in the computer field—while continuing to work at her current position. Her plan is to attend night classes to study selling and marketing.

Changes are difficult in any situation, but priority managers must take ownership of their priority, and this includes making changes when necessary.

ADJUST YOUR TIME FRAME

Monica is an assistant director of a mental health organization. Her priority is to learn how to help her clients become more independent and to eventually live on their own, rather than continue to live in residential homes. Monica's strategies include learning more about each client—their skills, interests, and abilities. Once she gathers this material, she meets with each client, and together they develop a plan. Since Monica works with clients who are former substance abusers, the long-term homeless, and mentally or emotionally challenged, she experiences many ups and downs in the attainment of her priority. Some days, clients show great progress; other days, they fall behind.

Monica, re-evaluating her priority, realized that it would take more time to reach her goal because she needed to be a coach to help her clients keep improving. After completing her priority evaluation, she decided to look at each client carefully, and if more time was needed to do this, she would extend the time frame. You might find that you, too, underestimated the length of time necessary to reach your priority, so be willing to reconsider your time frame and to give yourself sufficient time.

Audrey is an accounting manager of a jewelry retail chain. When she set a priority to help automate the company's records—including purchasing, shipping and receiving, sales, and administrative and asset management—she found her time divided between her normal accounting job and getting her priority set in motion. She spoke to her boss, Virginia, about the problem of having too much work and not enough time or resources to complete it. Virginia listened carefully, then responded, "We're counting on you to automate the company records, Audrey. But we can't afford to hire someone else to do your job, so you're going to have to find a way to keep up with both."

This was not the answer Audrey had hoped for, but she knew it had been her decision to take on the automation project and that she would have to follow through with her commitment. Her solution was to adjust her time frame.

ADJUST YOUR PEOPLE SKILLS

While it's true that you own your priority, the help of others is needed to make it happen. Because you need the assistance of other people, you need to show them how they can benefit from working with you. Your challenge is to get people involved. The way to do this is to try to see the best in people, to let them know you appreciate their skills, and that their efforts count.

FIGURE 9–1
Useful Information on Associates

Name	Leonard V. Fairly (Lenny)
Position	Transportation Mgr.
Address	601 Blossom Rd.
	Dallas, TX
Tel. #	201-496-6111
FAX #	201-496-6001
Children	(4)
Hobbies	Golf
Interests	Transportation of the Future, Astrology
Special Skills	Software skills

Sarah started out in the office at a national moving company. After a year, she was moved into the dispatching department, where her priority was to become head dispatcher. She tried to learn as much as possible about the drivers, customers, trucks, and equipment in order to make a major contribution to the department. She worked extra hours, even bringing work home every night, and tried to make as many friends at work as possible. To add to her knowledge of the business, she developed a database with the names of people inside and outside the organization who would give her information and ideas about how to make bigger and better contributions to her organization. Figure 9–1 gives an example of the information Sarah used for her database. In addition to the name, phone number, company, and title of each individual, she recorded some personal information about each. When she spoke with them, her conversation was not just businesslike and impersonal. Knowing, for example, that Leonard was an avid golfer, allowed her to express a genuine interest in the individual, not just what he could do for her. Sarah found that people were generally more receptive and willing to help her achieve her priority when she was able to begin the conversation in an informed, personal manner. Because of the database she developed, she was able not only to achieve her priority but also to make some valuable friendships that will be useful for all her future priorities.

Charlie, a sales coordinator of a large office furniture wholesaler, is in charge of supporting the other salespeople in his office. He decided to set a priority to work on a program to cut down excessive returns by working closely with sales representatives and customers. Although his original priority was to cut returns by 20 percent, he only succeeded in cutting them by 7 percent. Too many salespeople were uninterested in his priority.

Charlie adjusted his priority to 15 percent, and at the same time he implemented a new strategy: To increase profits, he and the salespeople concentrated on reselling returns as well as trying to determine if there was a pattern to these returns. When a return was resold to the customer, Charlie would call both the salesperson and the customer with a personal "thank you."

Gradually, Charlie realized that his salespeople are sensitive about returns and that success would only result when everyone worked together to achieve it. To help mend the priority fences, Charlie sent everyone involved with the returns priority a handwritten note of appreciation for their help.

It's a good idea to send thank-you notes at various stages of the priority strategy, not just at the end. People want to be recognized for their efforts. Send them to your boss if she or he gave you support. Send them to department managers who may have given you advice, help, or just the courage to keep moving closer to your priority. A phone call or short visit is another option. All politics are local; your best public relations tool is showing people that you notice and appreciate their abilities and their effort.

Adjust Your Attitude

Wayne, an architect, set up a priority of earning a 5 percent salary increase. He arrived at the office early each day, took on extra duties, helped out others in his department, trained new architects, and worked hard with customers and potential customers—in short, he worked as though he were a major stockholder in the business. When he received his annual review, he found out that he'd received only a 3 percent pay increase.

Wayne was upset with himself. Why had he fallen short of his priority? Why hadn't his superior work made him more visible? Did his boss or someone else have it in for him? Why had his strategies fallen short?

After doing some soul-searching and talking it over with his wife, Wayne decided that instead of worrying about how things could have been, he should put his energy to more positive use. He reviewed the written annual salary review and noticed the comment that he was trying to do too many different things, rather than taking on major duties and specializing in them.

Wayne decided he would try to learn more about his customers and make a special effort to get all of his jobs out on time. In addition, he sat down with his boss and together they outlined exactly what was expected of him and how he could best help the company. Rather than wasting his energy feeling sorry for himself, he learned from past mistakes and kept a positive attitude. Now, he works as hard as ever but in a more focused—and useful—way. His enthusiasm is greater also because he knows he is right on track to get his 5 percent raise. He also tried to keep a positive attitude and avoid excessive worrying by settling down to the work at hand. Wayne was excited again because he knew that this time he would successfully reach his priority.

Adjust Your Family and Personal Obligations

In some cases you may find that a business priority conflicts with a personal one. In these cases, it is especially important to come up with creative solutions to the problem. In many cases, you may find a single solution solves both problems.

Mary is a purchasing agent for a medical supply company. The job requires long hours and a great deal of traveling. Mary set a priority to become a purchasing supervisor, and with a combination of hard work and increased hours, she did it.

When Mary evaluated her priority, she found she hadn't fully involved her family. She decided that during the next priority she would involve them more so they could learn about her company and responsibilities. She decided that she would take her daughter and son to work occasionally, that she would attend more of the family functions the company offered, and that she would include her husband and family in more of her present and future priorities. Now, her entire family is part of her priority team. Rather than being resentful of lost quality time, they are eager to help her reach success. The kids do the dishes each night so she has an extra half hour to work. As a result, she is able to finish projects early and take an occasional day off to spend with her family.

Adjust Your Niche

Susan is a lawyer with a large law firm. When she began her career, she didn't know which specific area of law would hold her interest and help build her career. A number of years—and priorities—later, she looked at adjusting her priorities as a tool to help her find where she fit in the organization. She learned that she loved to manage projects; the more difficult the project, the better she is able to use her time and talents to deliver successful results. Recently, she became president of her law association.

Adjust All Priorities toward Your Number-One Priority

Patricia is a copywriter with a New York advertising agency whose major priority is to become the creative director for all the designers and writers in the agency. Her most recent priority is to get to know more of the designers and writers personally. To accomplish this, she is running seminars for them on the keys to successful campaigns.

Adjust Your Job into a Career

The people who will transform a job into a career are those who are able to adjust their priorities to help their organization. If you carefully adjust your priorities to fill your organization's needs, you will be seen as someone who can manage your work efforts to deliver important, and timely, contributions.

Joan, a supervisor with a large audiovisual service, wants to become manager of her department. While evaluating her priority, she found that her biggest problem was working with all the service technicians and customers while handling the various other duties of her job. She decided to make a list of each technician's most important skills and tried to give them assignments that would fully match their talents. As Joan developed her skills in matching people with specific jobs, she took a step closer to turning her job into a career.

Steve is the finance manager for a business equipment firm. His priority was to keep his position during a period when the company was having financial problems that

had led to downsizing. Steve did everything he was asked
to do for the company, which included a great deal of traveling as well as laying people off and closing some departments and plants.

Steve had not expected the additional work when he
originally set up his priority, but he adjusted his expectations and developed a reputation for going the extra mile.
When the time finally arrived for the company to decide
what managers they would retain, Steve made the cut,
showing people around him you can turn a job into a career as long as you're willing to give your priority 110 percent effort.

SEE THE BIG PICTURE

Achieving your priority requires that many factors, including those just described, are working together. Some people get overly upset when the results are not what they expected. They beat themselves up mentally, blaming
themselves for their lack of success, without reviewing the
factors they could not control.

Take Janet's example. As retail manager of a clothing
store, she is required to set a monthly sales quota. Month
after month, she was falling short. Janet got very upset
about this. Her doctor, who became convinced she was
headed for a nervous breakdown, told her to speak to her
boss about her concerns.

To Janet's surprise, her boss understood why her
monthly results were less than her forecast. Her boss told
her that the store was located in a high unemployment
area, and that the results were good under the circumstances.

Kevin is a stockbroker with a large investment company.
After evaluating his priority to increase his yearly sales by

10 percent, he found that he could conceivably increase sales by as much as 15 percent. He knew that all priorities are, at best, estimates of potential results and that with the right mental focus he could exceed them.

Kevin enjoyed his job when customers were happy with their investments, but he did not like facing customers to explain why their investments were sinking. He learned that part of his job was to educate his customers that there was no such thing as a guaranteed investment increase, that their investment might increase or decrease depending on the stocks they purchased. He also realized that even though he was working towards a new priority of a 15 percent increase in sales, additional factors, such as the economy, would play a role in its success.

Try to reach every priority you take on, but avoid putting excessive pressure on yourself that might impair your mental or physical health. Adjust your expectations to a realistic level, and look at everyday occurrences in relation to the larger scheme of things. What is most important today might seem trivial in a month.

Falling short of achieving your original priority does not mean you have failed. You have gained experience working with others; you have set, directed, and managed your priority; and you have learned the steps in the process.

Some people fear failure and try everything to avoid it, sometimes paying a high cost. Some even try to cover potential failure with dishonest acts. It's important to never take failure personally. Failure shows you're trying to reach success. Successful people learn how to succeed from their setbacks, making whatever adjustments are necessary.

SUMMARY

As organizations, circumstances, and, most importantly, you yourself change, you will need to make adjustments to your priority as necessary. Realize that some things are simply out of your control and that making an adjustment does not mean that you have failed. Instead, adjusting your priorities shows that you are looking at the big picture and directing your life where you want it to go rather than wasting time, effort, and energy on something that is no longer feasible for or important to you.

Chapter Ten

To the Finish Line

Successful people become that way through their ability and motivation to achieve their priorities. They develop a reputation for focused thinking and work even in difficult circumstances. Now that you have finished your priority evaluation and made the necessary adjustments, all that's left to do is to bring it to closure.

BRAINSTORMING

Cut down the time and effort necessary to finish your priority by coming up with ideas to really move ahead. When you think of an idea, jot it down, then *use* it. Call a meeting of the people who are part of your priority team or meet with close friends who are interested in giving you feedback to help you reach your priority.

Periodically review your file, compare the strategies listed there with the strategies you are currently using, and compare your performance with the performance you expected. Then determine what you must do *right now* to bring your priority across the finish line. First, brainstorm a list of ideas.

Michelle is a sales engineer whose number one priority is to write user manuals and give her customers more training on the new products, but with the shortage of people in her office, she has so far been unable to accomplish her priority. Figure 10–1 is Michelle's list of ideas for completing her priority.

FIGURE 10–1
Michelle's Ideas for Finishing Priority

- Get extra help from other departments.
- Hire temporary part-time help.
- Ask boss for extra time to finish.
- Hire trainer or consultant to write manual.
- Cut down on sales appointments and use time to finish.

Once you've made a list of your own like Michelle's, cross out the ideas you don't think will work and focus on those that are most likely to bring success. Record these ideas in a log on finishing your priorities, along with the action needed to turn these ideas into results.

BREAK THE HABITS THAT HOLD YOU BACK

Many priority managers find that one of the most difficult aspects of the priority process is bringing the priority to a close because they are caught up in habits that slow down their progress. For example, Stan, a financial assistant with a business management company, wants to become supervisor in his department. Doing this will require extra time and work to learn new systems and to take courses on management. But Stan spends much of his extra time either on the golf course or at the driving range. He made a contract with himself to cut down on golf and to use this time to focus on his career priority.

Corinne is an administrative group leader with a warehousing and distribution service. Her priority is to become manager of her department. She knows she will only be offered this position when she is able to take on projects that will help not only her department but her company, so she set a priority to determine why many packages are arriving at the warehouse in damaged condition and why others are opened and have contents missing.

In order to complete this priority, Corinne knew she needed to spend more time away from her desk, visiting the loading dock and observing the opening and counting of the hundreds of packages that arrive daily. She determined that she needed to spend at least two hours a day, more on the days when deliveries are heavy. Corinne moved from doing a desk job to becoming a very visible person within the organization, which will help her reach her priority of a management position.

AGE IS NO OBSTACLE

We live in a culture that focuses on youth. Below are statements by some priority attendees on the subject of age.

- "I just turned 40, and I want to go back to school at night to study auto mechanics."
- "I'm only 35, and I want to go into health care management."
- "I will turn 50 next year, but I want to go into accounting; I've always wanted to go into this field."
- "I feel my age and experience will help me get into the teaching field."
- "I would never have reached my latest priority without the maturity that came from raising a family on my own."
- "I'm not getting older; I'm getting more priority conscious, and my life is exciting again."
- "I can become all I want to be with the resources I've developed over the years and the knowledge of myself."

Use your age as an advantage. Experience and self-knowledge can be used to open doors. I enjoy the story of a 72-year-old man who is an active skier. He doesn't want to listen to people complimenting him. He recently said, "It's never too late to set a priority and reach it. I ski with a man who is 104 years old, and he started skiing at 92." Rather than delaying or abandoning a priority because you think you're too old, use your age as a springboard to success.

DEVELOP A SENSE OF URGENCY

If you want to bring your priority to a close, get it done *today*, not tomorrow. Developing a sense of urgency means you must regularly call the people associated with your priority, send letters and e-mail, and keep selling your priority and the reasons why you must complete it.

Barbara, a cost accountant with an apparel manufacturer, has a priority to develop a cost-cutting program for her organization. Her deadline is December 31. She is working with each department head in the company and going over all the expenses to determine whether or not some of them can be cut. During each meeting, Barbara stresses the fact that every dollar saved in expenses is a dollar profit for the organization. When a department head would cancel a meeting to review the expenses, Barbara would make it clear that the meeting had to be rescheduled as soon as possible because the input of the department heads was crucial to completion of the priority by December 31. Barbara found that the more information she offered about the priority and the deadline, the more help she received from others.

Sometimes a priority suffers because its originator must wait for a boss who lacks a sense of urgency to act on it. A priority is much too important to leave it to someone else to run interference for it and support it. Maintaining a sense of urgency must be part of your daily action plan, or your priority will lose valuable momentum.

WATCH YOUR DEADLINE

The successful priority manager stands out from the pack because of his or her ability to measure where the priority stands in relation to the deadline. Rather than just assuming you know where your priority stands, take the time to measure your progress and then determine what needs to be done to finish it.

A seminar leader once said, "The smartest person I ever met is my tailor. Every time I see him, he takes a new measurement." The tailor doesn't assume your waistline remains the same. Good tailors take the time to measure so that the shirt, coat, slacks, or suit will fit correctly.

Don't assume anything when it comes to your valuable priority. Once you determine where you are in relation to finishing it, review the main reasons why you set it up and then focus on the rewards to you and others when the priority is successfully completed. Now go forward with the necessary work to bring it to completion. Nothing makes you feel better in life than choosing a priority, setting a strategy in place, and then seeing all the pieces coming together. Visualize yourself as a victorious manager of your priority, receiving compliments from your friends, associates, and family for your hard work.

Ideally, you've set up the priority within a sufficient time frame to complete it, but sometimes you need to come into work earlier than normal or stay later for a week or two to complete it. The key is to bear down in the final stretch. Many priorities are diluted or abandoned because they never receive that final push.

Barbara, a technical writer, set a priority to finish a complicated employee manual for a customer within two weeks. Midway through the job, she realized she would not complete the project on time if she continued to work as she had been. To get ideas on ways to handle the problem, Barbara made a list of "what if" scenarios:

- What if I discussed the assignment with a co-worker?
- What if I locked my office door and stayed there until I finished?
- What if I reviewed the work so far and evaluated it fully?
- What if I threw all the work out and started over?
- What if I requested an extension?
- What if I worked on Saturday?
- What if I put some other priorities on hold until this is done?

Notice how the "what if" questions can help you to look at a priority from different angles and how it can become less threatening once you develop some options.

BE PERSISTENT

The winner's circle is filled with people who are willing to persist, even under the most trying circumstances. They fall down just like everyone else, but they get back up to reach for the priority again. Thomas Edison would often repeat an experiment thousands of times before he reached success. He claimed that each time he tried an invention and failed, he learned something more about the invention and himself and would go on to the next step a wiser person.

In the world of priorities, you will finish when you keep trying, going over all the steps, and then trying again to get closer to success. The top salespeople in the world are

women and men who are willing to ask for the order over
and over again. Keep selling others on the benefits of your
priority. When you persist, you succeed.

DON'T FEAR SUCCESS

Many priorities fail because of the way the priority seeker
views the priority. The problem is plain when he or she
says, "I'll finish the ABC report when I have time," or
"When I can reach an agreement with everybody in the department, I'll develop a marketing plan on the X409 wid-
get." Such statements, while trying to give the impression
that the person really wants to complete the priority,
merely offer excuses to postpone it.

Many people fear success. They know that finishing an
important priority will bring exposure, experience, and
recognition that will lead to future priorities. They will be
asked by others within the organization for assistance. You
have learned how to begin the priority process and how to
keep it going with your skills and strategies, using other
people and resources to bring it to a completion. You have
become an expert in priority management. Enjoy it fully.

Each priority you complete improves you and increases
your confidence in handling higher-level priorities. This
change is called *personal priority power* and is discussed in
greater detail in the next chapter.

SUMMARY

Once you have finished your priority evaluation and made
the necessary adjustments, the final step is to bring it to
completion. This is the most difficult part of all, and many
people spend energy that should be used to bring the priority to completion on making excuses as to why it isn't

finished. Rather than make excuses, spend your energy to complete the process. Come up with a list of ideas that will help you finish the project, then act on those ideas. Develop a sense of urgency. Create a log showing what you have done so far and what remains to be done, and keep an eye on the deadline. If time is running out, create a "what if" list to help you look at the project from all angles, then take the steps necessary—whether asking for help or spending more time—to complete the project. Most importantly, never give up. Remember, nobody plans to fail; they just fail to plan.

Chapter Eleven

Personal Priority Power

When you began taking action steps to achieve your priority, it is very likely that you did not realize the full extent of the benefits that achieving your priority would bring. When defining your priorities, you most likely only saw them in relation to their desired result. Successful priority managers know that the benefits of success usually exceed what they originally bargained for.

Take George's example. His priority was to quit smoking because he saw the direct benefits thereof: increase his health, save money, and so on. When he successfully quit, though, George realized that, along with the obvious benefits, there were many others that he never bargained for. He not only felt better and saved about $60 a month but also felt his personal confidence grow. Quitting was one of the hardest things he ever had to do, but he proved to himself that he had the strength and mental toughness to quit anyway. This confidence has carried over to all other aspects of his life. Now he has full confidence that he can do anything he sets his mind to. Things that once looked like huge obstacles he now sees as only minor roadblocks. Successfully completing one priority has given him confidence and ambition that will serve him well when facing all future priorities.

The rewards of bringing your priority to successful completion are far more than recognition from family, friends, and peers, or a possible promotion. The greatest reward is a new feeling about yourself. You may look the same, but deep inside a fundamental change has taken place that will influence the way you look at the world, relate to others, and feel about future priorities. This new or strengthened sense of self-esteem will play an important role in helping you overcome fears that may have previously slowed you down or affected the way you handle your priorities. Nothing succeeds like success; each priority you complete helps to cool the heat of your fears.

INCREASE YOUR PERSONAL PRIORITY POWER WITH PUBLIC RELATIONS

Priorities that succeed, or even those that almost make it, provide excellent opportunities to "toot your horn" to others in your field. You will generate excellent public relations for your priority and yourself when you take advantage of opportunities to present it to your supervisors or management as well as to the larger public.

Joe, an information specialist with a grocery firm, worked with a team of five on a quality control project. Once the priority was completed and the results were developed, the members of the team presented it to their bosses, employees, and other department managers to demonstrate its value. Each team member sent invitations to the people they wanted to attend. At the end of the presentation, which included a video and overhead transparencies, there was a question-and-answer session. Those who saw the presentation recognized the hard work and dedication that led to its success. As a result, Joe and each member of the team saw their value and reputation in the company rise dramatically. Supervisors and management recognize that Joe is a hardworking, intelligent, and dependable employee, and they frequently assign him the most important projects, knowing that the priorities are in good hands. In fact, Joe expects a promotion in the near future because he has established himself as a successful priority manager. Sharing the success of the priority through the presentation has led to more and more success for his career.

Let people know about you and your accomplishments regularly. Send your local editor a news release, which is simply a typed statement about your latest achievement: getting a promotion, winning a contest at work, completing a seminar, workshop, or college program, or anything else newsworthy. Be sure to clear the news release with your boss or public relations department before sending it. Then proofread it and mail or send it to the appropriate editor.

The people and companies you read about in the newspaper get that exposure by sending their information to the editor. The guests you see on TV talk shows get there by approaching the producers with information about themselves.

Once the news release appears, keep a copy in a safe place; you can use it later to develop a brochure on your achievements. Every article about you in newspapers or trade journals helps build your reputation and increases your personal priority power.

KNOW YOUR VALUE

In the world of finance and accounting, *net worth* is a basic term. Net worth is what the company or individual is worth right now with all of their assets sold for cash and all of their liabilities paid off. Net worth in terms of personal power means knowing your value to yourself and your organization as well as knowing your potential for increased value in the future. Answer the questions below on your perceptions of value.

1. How valuable do you feel after completing your priority?

_____

_____

_____

_____

2. Do you feel that others respect you and value you?

_____

_____

_____

_____

3. How do you feel about the value you now have in your work and personal life?

_____

_____

_____

_____

4. Name the things that make you feel good about yourself. What makes you a special person, with real value?

_____

_____

_____

_____

The real value of your successful priorities is the feelings you have about yourself. You begin to like and understand that person in the mirror. You know that you have certain liabilities you must work on, but you become a new person because you know you are valuable. Ideally, that feeling of self-esteem becomes a steady source of inspiration.

A student in one of my classes once said to me after class, "I know I have potential and value, but how do I break away from the rut my life is in right now?" We discussed the importance of matching talents and interests with specific priorities and looking at life as an exciting voyage, filled with opportunities. Become the manager of the priorities in your life by focusing on what you can become rather than on what you think you lack or cannot accomplish.

MANAGE YOUR FUTURE

Successful people know that the real value of completing a priority is the feeling of self-worth that results. You now have the opportunity to increase your success by selecting another priority. In the space below, list some of the priorities you would like to complete in the next week, month, or year. Don't limit yourself to strictly work or career; focus on personal priorities as well, such as running a marathon, learning to deep-sea dive, or meeting new people to enhance your social life. Remember, you are the manager of your priorities, and only you will steer the course of your future. Aim high and put the tips and techniques you have learned to work on accomplishing all the things you have so far only dreamed of.

Future Priorities

1. _____

2. _____

3. _____

4. _____

5. _____

6. _____

7. _____

8. _____

9. _____

10. _____

SUMMARY

Successfully completing a priority brings benefits above and beyond the desired and most obvious result. Overcoming obstacles and making your priority a reality gives you confidence in yourself—a huge asset when tackling future priorities. Success increases your personal power, and that feeling of self-esteem becomes a steady source of inspiration. Success snowballs, and this momentum can be used to accomplish anything on which you set your sights. Harness this power. Use your successes as the building blocks upon which you will lay the foundation for the future—the future as *you* want it to be.

Index